DEDICATION

I0101878

This book is dedicated to every reader who has spent time trying to fit in or change someone else — and to every poet, sage, artist, edge walker among us who has the audacity to stand in his or her otherness.

THE
OTHERNESS
FACTOR

Co-Creating and Sustaining

Intentional Relationships

KATHLEEN HALL △ BONNER HARDEGREE

THE OTHERNESS FACTOR

Co-Creating and Sustaining Intentional Relationships

A non-fiction book — some of the names and identifying details of people described in this book have been changed to protect their privacy.

Published by Collaborative Options LLC, Austin, Texas. Inquiries should be emailed to info@collaborativeoptions.com

ISBN: eBook: 978-0990390404
ISBN: Paperback: 978-0990390411

Cover Design: Mayapriya Long at Bookwrights
Cover Art: *An Ode to Charles Darwin* by Kathleen Hall

Disclaimer: This work represents the collective, selected knowledge of philosophers, poets, artists, scientists, psychologists — extraordinary men and women who were willing to look beyond the ordinary to consider the meaning of life, love and purpose. Although it is intended to open your hearts, minds and souls to become more of who you are, it is not intended to substitute for the services of qualified professionals. Very few of us are able to navigate these waters alone. Becoming who we are is a journey we take together.

I used to think I was the strangest person in the world but then I thought there are so many people in the world there must be someone just like me who feels bizarre and flawed in the same way I do. I would imagine her, and imagine that she must be out there thinking of me too. Well, I hope that if you are out there and read this and know that, yes, it's true I'm here and I'm just as strange as you.

—Frida Kahlo, Mexican Artist (1907–1954)

CONTENTS

PROLOGUE

Much has been written about our ability to use Source[1] energy to co-create our individual lives through the power of intention. Although the power of intention has been widely studied, we found little on the subject of *intentional relationships*. It seemed to us the cumulative effect of two or more people accessing the Source to co-create relationships held enormous promise. Could the power of intention help us achieve deeper, more meaningful and peaceful relationships? Would we stop exhausting ourselves trying to *fit in* or *change one another* in favor of honoring and exploring one another's *otherness*? Is it possible, by redefining and redirecting a more collaborative power of intention, we might witness the exponential effect of co-creation — leading to the transformation of the human network, creating healthier, more balanced and harmonious alliances based on both our *oneness* and our *otherness*?

———————————

In the following pages we observe the evolution and integration of science and spirituality. We witness the unfolding and merging of psychology, sociology and biology. The bright lines between these disciplines have begun to blur as we open ourselves to the possibilities of who we are as individuals and as a species.

When we began this work, the word *otherness* was fairly uncommon. Today, both the word and concept of *otherness* is gaining traction and respect. How do intention and otherness unfold and merge in individuals, relationships and communities?

This book will take you to places far beyond the ordinary and offer you the power, courage and audacity to stand in your own otherness. As you turn the page, invite new energy and insight. Expect to be surprised by the potency and durability of co-creating your life!

PART ONE |
GETTING OUT OF OUR WAY

CHAPTER ONE | **THE SOURCE**

Truth is the only religion; untruth is bondage.
—Mahatma Gandhi

From the beginning of time, humankind has been fascinated by the mystical nature of our existence. Most of us like the idea we are spiritual beings, but few of us seem comfortable with our numinous quality, let alone set out to enjoy it. What if our only job is to be 'more of who we are?' Would we know how?

Early Encounters

We were mesmerized. Sitting cross-legged on the living room floor, we could barely contain the kinetic anticipation, fascination and dread when a straight-laced man in a dark suit and skinny tie appeared on the screen and said, "You are about to enter The Twilight Zone." His name was Rod Serling and the program, *The Twilight Zone*, introduced us to stories about people confronted with unexplained experiences, visions and encounters from other dimensions. In spite of its otherworldly, fictional nature, there was something sweetly intimate and familiar about the experience of limitlessness.

For centuries, great philosophers, scientists and teachers have referenced hidden forces and unexplained events as they probed the meaning of human existence. Almost all religions, both eastern and western, as well as ancient belief systems, refer to a mystical power that affects this world and our human experience. We know this mystical power as God, Oneness, Higher Consciousness, Divine Intelligence, Intent, Field of Intention, Atman, Buddha, Ultimate Reality, the *Source*, soul, spirit — any name used to express the spiritual essence of one's true nature.

Spiritual journeys are uniquely personal and religious beliefs and practices are often part of an individual's pursuit of truth. Committed to honoring our unique *otherness* and differing world views, we encourage you to let your spirit roam with curiosity as we explore what thought leaders over the ages have discovered about the Source and its influence on our lives and relationships.

Beliefs, Barriers and Bridges

Where do our beliefs come from? Certainly, there are observable scientific laws that are easy to experience and validate. But, when it comes to belief systems about ethics, morals, religion and faith, beliefs are ultimately about choice. In the New Testament, the apostle Paul said, "Faith is the substance of things hoped for, the evidence of things not seen" (Hebrews 11:1). When a belief is based on faith, we imagine something beyond our capacity to observe, prove or validate.

Yet, most beliefs begin in childhood, long before we understand such concepts or have the ability to discern for *ourselves*.

Do you recall the crazy things some of us accepted as truth? *My mother warned me against swallowing watermelon seeds, suggesting one would grow in my stomach. I can't tell you how many summer nights I spent with my hand over my stomach, waiting, watching!* How much of what we heard as children still guides our actions? Have old adages influenced and affected our authenticity? Do we attract more attention with honey than vinegar? Are white lies innocent? How much of what we heard as children serves as barriers or bridges to understanding ourselves, and how we relate to others?

Later in life, during times of vulnerability or life crises, we are sometimes compelled to look for reasons beyond our ability to comprehend. Often, this search leads to major shifts in our belief system or an *awakening*, which deconstructs the world we once knew.

A Case of Mistaken Identity

I was well into my fifties when I began to question many of the fundamental concepts and beliefs I had relied upon my entire life. By all outward accounts, I was successful. My second wife and I had been married for almost 14 years, raising her three children and providing for my three from an earlier marriage. We lived on a million-dollar ranch near Austin, Texas. I was a successful businessman and entrepreneur. My wife and children drove late-model luxury cars and took expensive vacations. In the community, I was president of the local school board and an active member of my church. I thought I had done everything right, providing for my family, worshipping my God. Yet, I felt empty, haunted by what I began to realize was a loveless marriage and a meaningless career. I no longer recognized the person in the mirror.

For almost three years I experienced a sometimes brutal and radical transformation as everything I believed in began to dissolve, like old fabric crumbling in my hand. My marriage ended in divorce, my company went bankrupt and many of my friends abandoned me. I suffered through dark nights of depression and hopelessness.

Feeling naked, stripped of my status and standing in the community, I began to rediscover my spiritual core. My loneliness led to a quieter, deeper connection to my soul. I read, studied and formed a discussion group with other spiritual pilgrims. I traveled to jungles, mountaintops, riverbanks, to learn from indigenous tribes, shamans and other thought leaders. I began writing.

I deconstructed and began rebuilding my belief system based on a deeper, more personal, and I think, spiritual foundation. As difficult as this journey has been, I am convinced that I woke up from a case of mistaken identity. I don't regret my first 50 plus years – they were filled with the excitement and challenges of growing into manhood, the excruciatingly tender experiences of learning to be a father. I am, however, grateful for the transformation to awareness; to consciously live my life, explore my spirituality and express my love from a less ego-driven place.

—Bonner

Beliefs as a Road Map

Beliefs provide a road map for our lives — building bridges or constructing barriers to achieving our fullest potential. By the time we reach adulthood, most of us have developed fairly tenacious egos. Because we want to be affirmed, accepted and included by others, we look for evidence to support our beliefs. We develop allies and surround ourselves with people who have similar convictions. If you grew up in a community with common religious, political or social beliefs, you know from personal experience this can be a powerful, cohesive force. Common beliefs become a structure for acceptance, and indeed, acceptance by others is highly valued by our egoist — fabricated, false — selves. In the realm of the mystical, ideas tend to be more abstract, often in conflict with family or community beliefs — here it takes spiritual courage to embrace the unknown or unfamiliar.

When beliefs change, our egoist self sets out to find new allies and support. However, even among allies, there are always differences to challenge one another's thinking. In *The Road Less Traveled*,[2] M. Scott Peck tells us, "The path to holiness lies through questioning everything."

Consider your own bridges and barriers. How have your beliefs changed along the way? Is your road map taking you where you want to go?

Taking the Road Less Traveled

With gratitude to Robert Frost whose poem gave life to this phrase and to M. Scott Peck who wrote the archetypal book on love and spirituality, *The Road Less Traveled*, we continue along this less traveled road for many reasons, but one in particular: The journey to intentional relating is more about *why not* than *how to*!

Millions of "how to" books are sold every day telling us how to lose weight without diet and exercise, how to find the love we deserve, ten easy steps to joy and happiness! We are fragile, sometimes desperate, consumers looking for love, acceptance and fulfillment. No well-traveled road exists for building or finding the relationship we long for and deserve. On the road less traveled, we ask *why not?* —knowing our access to Source energy will provide the power, wisdom and love we need to form relationships we can only now just imagine.

To find the road less traveled, to summon the power of intention and create harmony in our lives and relationships, we need to challenge our current belief systems, including our self-imposed ponderous limitations, expectations and egoist fears. The *why not* is about being awake and aware, about getting to know our true selves.

There are many compelling and competing scientific theories, spiritual tenets and mystical signals to capture our attention and challenge our thinking about who we are and how we evolve as human beings. In our collaboration, we were not surprised to discover we have differing beliefs. However, we share some fundamental principles that underscore our confidence in humankind's ability to form and sustain intentional relationships from a state of awakened, evolving consciousness and love-based volition:

- The universe, and everything in it, is energy (also referred to as consciousness). We view matter as energy in motion. Nobel Laureate, Max Planck proclaimed this phenomenon at the beginning of the 20th century and it continues to be confirmed as science delves deeper into the quantum physics theories first advanced by Planck.
- There is order, balance and harmony in the way the universe functions. One cannot look at the interconnection of life and life systems on this planet and not

be convinced it is a well-ordered, interdependent and intelligent system.

- We rediscover our true essence, not through a linear journey, but through an interior, cyclical, spiritual journey. Beliefs continue to evolve as we discover our Source energy and the relativity of our experience.

Thought Leaders, Meta Physicists and Mystics

Over the ages, thought leaders have provided us spiritual guidance and inspiration. These pilgrims include poets, sages, saints, philosophers, psychiatrists, scientists, ministers, artists and paupers. Jesus, Mahatma Gandhi, Voltaire, Mother Teresa, Walt Whitman, Albert Einstein, Carl Jung, to name just a few. Although these light bearers were influenced by different religions, cultures, professions and life's experiences, each revealed a relationship with a higher power, a faith in the mystical nature of our existence.

Over two hundred years before the birth of Christ, Aristotle, considered by many as one of the most inspired thinkers in history, and the person most often regarded as the father of physics, realized there were things that could not be explained through a careful and scientific analysis of the physical world. He called it "the other physics," which we know today as "metaphysics."

Today, modern scientists recognize that in the extended physical world — the cosmos and the intricate realms of the sub-atomic world — the lowest common denominator is not matter but energy. In the cosmos, astrophysicists have determined that 'black holes' are actually filled with dark or non-light-emitting energy. In the sub-atomic world, quantum physicists explore the fabric of minute structures that form matter and uniformly acknowledge that when viewing the world through the lens of quanta, what they measure is empty space filled with energy. It seems we are, after all, energy receivers and transmitters. As Yoda might say, *just lovable little bundles of energy are we!*

For centuries, knowledge, wisdom and inspiration were passed on by spoken or written words. This same information is now flying through cyberspace, touching the hearts and minds of millions in our global community. How do we begin to reconcile the wealth of knowledge, wisdom and inspiration among and between our different cultures, religions and languages?

One effort at reconciliation began in the mid 1980s with the formation of an international, interreligious council, 'The Snowmass Conference.' This council was originally formed to promote dialogue, improve understanding and explore spiritual practices across different religious traditions with the hope of creating a forum to address spiritual as well as worldwide social and economic issues.

Thomas Keating, a Trappist monk and founder of an international organization dedicated to reclaiming the Christian tradition of contemplative prayer and the mystical theology that supports this type of prayer[3], gathered fifteen of the world's religious leaders at 'The Snowmass Conference' and formulated agreements entitled *The Guidelines for Interreligious Understanding: Points of Agreement or Similarity*[4] defining eight points of agreement on the subject of spirituality. These agreements are an epochal achievement when we consider the number of wars and lives lost in the name of religion — a positive shift in recognizing our collective consciousness, our oneness:

1. The world religions bear witness to the experience of Ultimate Reality to which they give various names: Brahman, Allah, (the) Absolute, God, Great Spirit.
2. Ultimate Reality cannot be limited by any name or concept.
3. Ultimate Reality is the ground of infinite potentiality and actualization.
4. Faith is opening, accepting and responding to Ultimate Reality. Faith in this sense precedes every belief system.
5. The potential for human wholeness — or other frames of reference, enlightenment, salvation, transformation, blessedness, nirvana — is present in every human person.
6. Ultimate Reality may be experienced not only through religious practices but also through nature, art, human relationships, and service of others.
7. As long as the human condition is experienced as separate from Ultimate Reality it is subject to ignorance, illusion, weakness and suffering.
8. Disciplined practice is essential to the spiritual life; yet spiritual attainment is not the result of one's own efforts, but the result of the experience of oneness (unity) with Ultimate Reality.

Discussion

Bonner: *These Agreements are extraordinary! In spite of widely differing belief systems and church dogma, they acknowledge that Ultimate Reality may be experienced 'through nature, art, human relationships, and service of others.' How do you experience your spiritual path?*

Kathleen: *For me, my spiritual path is not about progression — it is more about rediscovering my true essence. Path sounds like there is some particular way we reach that discovery. I think each person's spiritual journey is unique. Rather than linear, my experience has been a cyclical, interior journey. In fact, I keep learning the same things over and over again!*

For example, I tend to be irreverent about life's many dramas, which keeps me from getting lost in someone else's story — but this irreverence can and does interfere with my ability to be an empathic listener. Perhaps this relearning is more about refining the balance between my otherness and oneness, as I try to become more aware of how I relate to others in a way that is both authentic and kind.

Bonner: *As we talk about our oneness — or 'consciousness' — we realize consciousness is a word with many different meanings. How do you define it?*

Kathleen: *I like William Tiller's explanation. He says, 'Reality is the form we give consciousness — that pure spirit equals pure consciousness — they are one and the same.*[5]

Bonner: *How then do you move from this understanding to Source energy? What in your experience suggests or convinces you there is Source energy or the power of intention?*

Kathleen: *To me, the Source and Consciousness (with a capital C) are one and the same. Early on, I was influenced by Mary Baker Eddy's mind over matter approach to life. I know I have the power to co-create my life by intending the outcome. Do we dream first, firing our neuro-transmitters, generating energy and activity, creating the dreamed reality? I think so. Little things like thinking of someone I haven't seen in a long time and having them call. Big things like seeing myself heading up a HR organization in a large hospital in Texas and finding myself in that position a few years later. In this latter case, I was living in Michigan with no thoughts or desire to move anywhere.*

Bonner: *Is there a key characteristic of Source energy that lets you know when you are acting with intention?*

Kathleen: *Initially, I feel a quickening sensation in my solar plexus, as if I am a Geiger counter, or perhaps more interestingly, a divining rod. I then experience an impeccable calm, sensing my oneness with all living things.*

Bonner: *Are you able to detect a difference between using intention to co-create life as opposed to successful drive and determination?*

Kathleen: *When I'm striving, with drive and determination, I feel agitated and stressed. My solar plexus constricts and I know I'm out of sync with my true nature. When I'm acting with intention, there is a sense of calmness and a quiet unfolding.*

Bonner: *So there's a tactile difference between these experiences!*

In addition to religious leaders, a growing number of contemporary writers are dedicated to exploring our spiritual evolution. Wayne Dyer's seminal book, *The Power of Intention*, is an excellent compilation of the work of thought leaders — physicists and mystics who have contributed to our knowledge about the power of intention and Source energy. Dr. Dyer frames our role in this relationship by stating, "We are not physical beings having a spiritual experience; rather, we are spiritual beings having a human experience."

At times, our mind over matter experiences have led to the notion we can affect everything in our life through the *power of intention* or the *power of attraction*. On the talk show circuit, this notion has been translated to mean we can access Source energy to acquire whatever we want, including designer shoes, new homes, expensive cars, yachts — a cornucopia of consumer goods. Although we understand and appreciate the power of attraction and the energetic relationship between thought and action, mind and body, our discussion of Source energy is about the journey of discovering our spiritual natures while learning to live, love and form relationships with intentionality. Similar concepts, different focus!

Shamans, Sorcerers and Scientists

In spite of some debate among anthropologists and mystics, Carlos Castañeda continues to be regarded as one of the finest metaphysical thinkers, spiritual anthropologists and writers of the last 50 years. In his work, *The Active Side of Infinity*, Castañeda tells the story of becoming a student and protégé' of a Yaqui Indian nagual named Don Juan Matus. As the protagonist in this work, Castañeda was captivated by the powerful effects of living life connected to Source energy, stating:

In the Universe there is an immeasurable, inde-
scribable force which shamans call intent and abso-
lutely everything that exists in the entire cosmos is
attached to intent by a connecting link. Sorcerers
are not only concerned with understanding the connecting link but they are concerned with cleansing it
of the numbing effects of living at ordinary levels of
consciousness

The force the shamans call *intent* is the Source. Sorcerers, as
used in this context, are not magicians, but individuals who
have become aware of Source energy and use it as a guiding
life force.

Although many view science as exacting in its objective and
impersonal methodology, Albert Einstein offered:

The most beautiful and profound emotion we can
experience is the sensation of the mystical. It is the
sower of all true science. He (or she) to whom this
emotion is a stranger, who can no longer wonder and
stand rapt in awe, is as good as dead.

The union of science and spirituality is becoming a more
common occurrence. Importantly, quantum physicists have
discovered compelling theoretical and empirical evidence
of our ability to co-create and change reality! We, Bonner
and Kathleen, were privileged to meet with William Tiller,
PhD, of the film *What the Bleep Do We Know?* Dr. Tiller,
a renowned physicist, left academia to more vigorously
explore consciousness as an innate power. As co-creators
of reality, Dr. Tiller believes we possess the ability to affect
not just our perception of reality, but to alter physical matter through the power of conscious energy. Many in the

scientific community have expressed a growing awareness and acknowledgement that we possess the ability to actively co-create our experience.

What Is Intention?

A number of thought leaders, spiritual pilgrims and quantum physicists have defined intention:

- Wayne Dyer, from his book *The Power of Intention*:

  The Source, which is intention, is pure, unbounded energy vibrating so fast that it defies measurement and observation. It's invisible, without form or boundaries. So, at our Source, we are formless energy, and in that formless vibrating spiritual field of energy, intention resides.[6]

- Wayne Teasdale, from his book *The Mystic Heart*:

  Divine consciousness possesses complete understanding. . . . Everything is part of an undivided wholeness where each being, or each conscious spirit, reflects the totality. . . . This totality is boundless, self-subsistent love.[7]

- William Tiller, PhD., quantum physicist from the film *What the Bleep Do We Know?*:

  Intentionality is the path to creation. I am much more than I think I am. I can influence my environment, people, space itself, my future.[8]

Each of these definitions reflects the power and force of intention. For the purpose of co-creating and sustaining intentional relationships, we offer the following definition to guide us on this journey:

> Intention is the ability to use our consciousness and volition to co-create our experiences in life by connecting to Source energy. A divine resource, Source energy is available to each of us whether we choose to access it or not.

Choosing an Intentional Life

When we choose to live an intentional life, we give up the ego-laden fantasy that we are separate from one another. We embrace the reality of our connection to all living things, and as we discard the cloak of fear, we recognize we are one with the Source and have the power to co-create our lives with intent.

Whether we choose to act with intention or not, our experience is a manifestation of energy. If I manifest love, I will co-create love in my life. If I manifest anger, I will co-create anger in my life. I become the person I manifest and what I manifest affects others within my created reality. We are one consciousness, one spiritual body, with the ability to co-create our individuated human experience.

To be clear, we all co-create our lives. If we do it with intention, we do it with coherence and clarity. Without the coherence of intention, our random, ego-driven lives are subject to wild swings of emotion — causing fear, despair and disappointment.

When we awaken to our boundless Source energy, we begin to open the portals of love, compassion and sensitivity. We discover our oneness, embrace our otherness, and experience our individual wholeness. No longer expecting someone else to 'complete' us, we are better prepared to enter a relationship with intentionality.

How will you live your life? How will you enter a relationship? The choice is yours.

CHAPTER TWO I
THE INNER TERRESTRIAL JOURNEY

Darkness embraces me
in the secret of night
and I AM.
Introspective,
I find life
stirring
to escape
the superficial bonds
that make me
the daytime me,
that I am not.
—Kathleen Hall

In Chapter One we introduced the idea that we may not know how to be more of who we are, because we haven't been paying attention to what we believe, or why we do what we do. Often, we seem to be on autopilot, moving through life, trying to fit in, please others and find our place. What if we moved through life with a greater sense of awareness and clarity? What if we discovered our lifework is not about fitting in or pleasing others?

We begin this discussion by recognizing our interior journey is a first step in the universal and ancient quest to find meaning in our existence. Although some may find this quest daunting, we believe there is a way to honor the vastness, majesty and brilliance of our physical and metaphysical world, and our own unique experience, without taking ourselves too seriously. Now is the time to get acquainted with our bundle of energy!

Tripping the Light Fantastic

It is almost surreal to step outside our homes and realize we live on a tiny planet orbiting the sun in a universe estimated to be between 12 and 14 billion years old. With the help of the Hubble Telescope, astronomers know our universe is expanding at accelerated rates of speed, with dark energy comprising more than 70% of the total universe. Although scientists haven't yet determined the exact nature of dark energy, they know it uniformly fills otherwise empty space.

In 2018, The James Webb Space Telescope (an infrared orbiting space observatory) is scheduled to replace the Hubble as our eye to the universe. This telescope will be sited one million miles away and provide 100 times more power than the Hubble. Scientists tell us the Webb Telescope will allow us to *see* new universes being formed and perhaps, help us *discover* intelligent life on other planets, on other universes![9] Does this sound a little like the Twilight Zone?

Since the beginning of recorded history, humankind has had an ongoing curiosity about the external world, including outer space. With each new extraordinary scientific discovery, we are captivated by possibilities, imagining how this new knowledge relates to our purpose, our reason for being.

With the advent of the Internet and a more accessible global community, we are brought to our knees by images and stories demonstrating the power of the human spirit, the capacity of the mind and depth of the soul. Although we navigate interior journeys alone, these shared Internet revelations are both personal and universal.

Our connection to all life is an immutable fact. As modern creatures, we are beginning to understand the complexity of our physical nature, the double helix DNA strands that form the blueprint of our bodies, our bio-suits, our physical individuation. In addition to this, we are cosmically connected to all life — possessing a spiritual DNA that links us to all that ever was or ever will be. In his book *Immortal Diamond*, Richard Rohr offers:

> You (and every other created thing) begins with a divine DNA, an inner destiny as it were, an absolute core that knows the truth about you, a blueprint tucked away in the cellar of your being, an 'imago Dei' that begs to be allowed, to be fulfilled, and to show it self.

Through Source energy, we share the collective wisdom, knowledge and potentiality to express our highest spiritual calling.

Before the Quest

The quest to understand the meaning of our existence and the interrelationship between humans, the universe and our deities appears to be primal. What motivates us to seek meaning?

Many of us have experienced the craziness of doing the same thing over and over, expecting a different result! Why do we cling to patterns of behavior that consistently yield the same kinds of conflicts, disappointments and despair? Is it because we keep looking for an external fix? What are we hoping to find? Do we know?

Through our personal experience and conversations with others, we've discovered this madness is often about trying to fill what we perceive to be an empty space within us, looking for something or someone to make us whole. Equally dysfunctional is the time we spend trying to win love, approval and acceptance — as if this were a contest. The irony is that many of us don't know what belief systems motivate us or what we hope to find. Yet, we seem determined to look externally to feel good and ease the pain of separateness, loneliness.

At some point along the way, we begin to realize this sense of incompleteness is driven by our egos. This nebulous self-awareness is wonderfully expressed by a caricature of a woman holding her forefinger to her temple with the caption: "I have always wanted to be somebody, now who the hell was it?"

A Glimpse in the Mirror

The day I composed this Chapter's poem, I was twenty-one years old, married to my high-school sweetheart, with an active 22-month old daughter and newborn son. That morning, I caught a glimpse of myself in the mirror while I was scouring the bathroom. The image surprised me and frightened me a little. Who was this person in the flowered moo-moo, toilet brush in hand; standing in a HUD subsidized condominium with shiny wood floors, sparkling windows, with a husband and two children? What strange, otherworldly forces had conspired to drop me here?

Let's take a look. The year was 1967 and, in spite of my mystical experiences as a child and propensity for non-compliance, my belief system included a fairly traditional expectation to marry and bear children before I became an old-maid at twenty-five. How would I survive without a husband to take care of me, and children to support me in my old age? How would I gain acceptance, affirmation and love if I failed to become the adult I was expected to become, to do what I was expected to do – to please others?

I had to grab the rose-covered cottage with the picket fence before it was too late! I was nineteen years old and pregnant when I married that cute boy 'I fell in love with' at sixteen.

—Kathleen

This story may sound absurd, it was the 1960s, a time of making love, not war. A time when women's liberation was changing the rules and freeing girls from such limited thinking. But, here we are, almost fifty years later — with bright, talented, single men and women still constructing their realities on similar, fictional belief systems about love, marriage, relationships and pleasing others. If not literally, many of us have figuratively caught glimpses of ourselves in the bathroom mirror, wondering who we are, why we feel so lost and alone.

Discussion

Bonner: *How did your life change after you glimpsed yourself in the mirror?*

Kathleen: *I had a small awakening. I think I am destined to have many small awakenings rather than the* big bang. This was the point when I renewed my relationship with mysticism and self-discovery. Life, in its perfect synchronicity, soon led me to a beautiful medium who reconnected me with my father and invited me to The Spiritual Life Center in Dearborn, Michigan. Penny Nichols, a gifted medium and spiritual teacher, led this center. I spent two years in the company of mediums as a student and apprentice.

Bonner: *I'm curious, how did your young husband and other family members feel about you consorting with mediums?*

Kathleen: *I learned at a very young age to keep this part of my life secret. But, in spite of my history, I tried to discuss it with my husband. He did not want to hear anything more about it, and if I'm not mistaken, he forbade me from meeting with them again. This was the 1960s, and although witches were no longer burned at the stake, I had a good sense of self-preservation. I went underground.*

Bonner: *At this point, how clear were you about your beliefs and your own guidance system?*

Kathleen: *I was a mess. I was compartmentalizing my life. I was strong enough in my spiritual beliefs to go underground and preserve this important aspect of my life. For the most part, I gave no thought to the cultural influences of my belief system, other than my activism for world peace and an end to the Vietnam War. I was on autopilot — with no conscious awareness that an unidentified system of beliefs was propelling me through life.*

Bonner: *What made you feel whole?*

Kathleen: *I was an insecure twenty-one-year-old woman with a high school diploma looking outside myself for approval, affirmation and love. I looked to my husband to make me feel loved and suffered disappointment when he did not behave in a way I thought husbands were supposed to behave. Looking back, I'm sure he felt equally disappointed when I did not behave in a way he thought wives were supposed to behave. I looked to my children to make me feel complete and confirm my ability to be a good mother. Thankfully, they had minds of their own! Today, I am less likely to look externally for approval, affirmation and love. If I do, I'm usually quick to call myself on it and look at the belief that sent me there.*

Bonner: *It sounds like you are learning to get out of your way.*

Kathleen: *It's a full time job!*

Getting Out of Our Way

Each of us will discover our truth, our spiritual essence, and connect to the Source in our own unique way. Some of us may experience a spontaneous awakening like Eckhart Tolle.[10] Others will experience a number of smaller, episodic awakenings over a lifetime. Regardless of how we awaken to our true selves, most of us will continue to be tested over and over again.

Although we reach our awakening in different ways, we have the opportunity to prepare ourselves by living a life of awareness. When we are aware — or present — we gain self-knowledge and develop the capacity to act with greater authenticity, maintaining integrity between our actions and beliefs. Conditioning our minds to act with this level of awareness is helpful as we begin the process of recognizing and quieting the ego (the subject of Chapter Three). Then, as we become more whole, we begin to recognize our own awakenings.

> The potential for human wholeness — or other frames of reference, enlightenment, salvation, transformation, blessedness, nirvana — is present in every human person.

> —5th Guideline[11]

Human wholeness — what does this look like, feel like? Most of us know what it is *not* as we look externally to find the love, purpose, meaning, stimulation or alchemy to fill that empty space to make us whole. What's missing in our lives? Before we can explore what's missing, we need to understand what's there.

Challenging Our Beliefs

Our beliefs are dominant, renegade influences on the quality of our life, guiding our perspective, sense of self and personal power. Unchecked, these cultural, social and religious belief systems are reinforced by unconscious, patterned behavior and become more limiting and imposing. Like race horses with blinders running a well-worn, familiar course, we get lost in our own tracks – not seeing or considering other ways of experiencing life and being in this world.

When we feel stuck, confused or off-balance, it's time to look at the rote belief(s) that sent us to these feelings.

By a process of inquiry we can *reconsider* our worldview through the following set of questions:

1. Why do I believe this is true?
2. Is it a self-imposed expectation about reality?
3. How does this expectation limit me, or my options?
4. What would my life be like if I did not hold this expectation?

As we examine our beliefs, we will uncover expectations that have *limited* our choices and opportunities. For example, we may find we have operated under a belief that: *real artists/musicians/writers/poets/actors* (fill in the blank) *are professionally trained/possess advanced degrees/come from artistic families* (fill in the blank) — which has the effect of limiting choices and opportunities. Or, we might operate under a belief we: *lack the social skills/looks/contacts* (fill in the blank) *to get the job/find love/get published* (fill in the blank). These expectations and limitations may be the result of a cultural, social or religious belief — or a belief based on an errant comment by an angry parent, friend or partner! Most of us have spent far too many years wrangling *old insults* carried as beliefs.

Whenever beliefs stifle our boundless energy and love, we are operating under the whims of ego — rationalizing based on phantom belief systems we have not revisited in decades. Now is the time to take off the blinders and stop getting lost in our own tracks!

Retooling Our Guidance System

Awareness, self knowledge and wholeness requires we understand our existing guidance system — a system we have constructed based on beliefs — which, of course, leads to our thoughts, behaviors and the quality of our life experiences. Many of us haven't paid much attention to why we think what we think or do what we do. As a result, we allow anonymous beliefs to guide our actions. What if we were more aware? What if we could retool this system and eliminate the layers of *other-imposed* or *self-imposed* beliefs that distract us from the essence of our true selves? What would our lives be like if we got out of our way?

We begin learning our cultural myths at birth, laying the foundation for a story we will continue to reenact over and over again. When we look within, we discover much of our guidance system is built and maintained by forces, factors and personalities outside of ourselves. These kinds of myths survive generations in the telling and retelling. The story may change as time passes, but the recurrence of the story becomes embedded in the structure of a culture: communities, families, work places and of course, individual guidance systems. Whether we are aware of it or not, many of our life experiences are based on myths. And, not surprisingly, myth is the mother lode when it comes to relationships and conflict.

Consider the implications. Are you viewing your life's drama as a spectator? How would you feel if you were fully present and engaged?

To retool our guidance system, we need to pay attention to what guides us. We hold many beliefs. Some we will choose to keep because they serve us well and reflect our own, conscious truth. Other beliefs will surprise us or, perhaps, frighten us! Once we begin examining our beliefs, we are better able to trust our deeper instincts, intuition and emotions.

Debunking Myths

To be clear, we all have myths to debunk. This awareness and subsequent self-discovery can be wonderfully liberating. Like cleaning the attic, we will discover old treasures worth saving among yellowed books, rotting fabric and dust motes.

Debunking myths isn't easy, but operating under myths leads to confusion and despair. We see retooling our guidance system as a step toward self-awareness. When we discover more about who we are, what we believe and why we do what we do, we will be in a better position to become the kind of person we want to attract into our lives. Let's look at some basic myths that fictionalize our lives:

a. *We fall in love, marry and live happily ever after.*
b. *Success is having a good job and making a good living.*
c. *If you work hard you will get ahead.*
d. *Being popular is important.*
e. *Attractiveness is driven by youth, appearance and vitality.*
f. *When we age, we become invisible, voiceless and idle.*
g. *Busy social schedules lead to happiness.*
h. *Clothes make the person.*
j. *Others?*

What myths are you holding on to? Do you want to let them go?

As you can imagine, the force of our cultural myths is powerful and pervasive. Many of us grew up under rigid belief systems or church doctrines that contributed to our sense of powerlessness; thinking we are unworthy, even when we know, in the deepest recesses of our soul, we are love.

If we don't debunk our myths, we continue to attract people into our life who reinforce these fictional stories. We then risk passing these myths on to our children. And so the pattern repeats.

Our guidance system has been forming from the moment we took our first breath. Not until we become aware of our unconscious thoughts, behaviors and beliefs, and retool them, will we consciously be able to co-create the life and world we want to inhabit.

Discussion

Kathleen: *The force of cultural myths is powerful and pervasive. In fact, it seems people go along to get along — yet relationships aren't working in spite of our attempts to conform to social norms and common behaviors. What about this myth?*

Bonner: *This myth is mindless. What's the point of going along to get along if in the end we feel empty, unsatisfied and resentful? When we create a guidance system that values avoiding conflict at all costs, we spend most of our time doing what we think other people want or expect us to do — and, as we know, it's all guesswork!*

Kathleen: *It is all guesswork — and, it seems, the costs are high.*

Bonner: *Well, let's look closely at this dynamic. If our sense of self-worth or identity is tied to whether or not we think others accept us, then the converse must also be true — when we're not accepted, we feel horrible about who we are. This belief gives others control of our sense of wellbeing or despair. These distractions pull us around by the nose. Rather than our guidance system guiding us, the system is misaligned to respond to someone else's expectations or demands.*

Kathleen: *Which makes me wonder about the people we attract into our lives.*

Bonner: *Without an updated guidance system, we will continue to do the same things and attract the same kind of people into our lives. If we aren't attracting the kind of people we want in our life — friends, partners, colleagues (family falls into a little different category here) — it's time to act with awareness, shift our beliefs and retool our guidance system. What I've observed and experienced is we tend to focus all our energy on trying to remake the person we're with, rather than encouraging him or her to become more of who they are. We need to get rid of the notion if THEY changed OUR life would be better. We have a choice here. We can either continue this futile effort to control others with our lock-step attitudes or do something that is going to effect a positive and lasting change in our life.*

Kathleen: *Trying to please or trying to change others is a path I walked for far too many years!*

Awareness and Authenticity

Becoming one with the Source is the ultimate quest, and as we've observed, this awakening may occur spontaneously or episodically over many years. Each person's journey is uniquely his or her own, with no right or wrong way — it's different for everyone.

But, unlike the *active* volition of living with awareness, connection to the Source requires the *passive* volition of allowing our connection — surrendering to our true essence. We have the ability to condition our mind and soul through practices that lead to living with greater awareness. A first step is getting to know who we are. When we become aware of our beliefs, assess and retool our guidance system, begin identifying and debunking the myths, we are on our way to living with awareness and giving up the roles we play.

Carlos Castañeda said it in plain language, "We either make ourselves happy or miserable. The amount of work is the same."

Is it really this simple? We think so. Moment-to-moment we have the opportunity to co-create our reality with or without intention. How we respond to multiple stimuli is ours to choose. Unlike the amoeba being poked in a Petri dish, we are sentient beings and have the absolute, ongoing option of choosing joy over sorrow, love over fear. It is up to us!

With awareness, we also assume greater responsibility to act with authenticity by maintaining integrity between our beliefs and what we do and/or say. So, what are the ways to make the transition from ego-driven, unconscious guidance systems to living with greater awareness and authenticity?

We have identified a few active volition practices that work for us. By this, we don't mean to convey we have 'succeeded' in living with awareness and acting with authenticity. To the contrary, we still have very active, tenacious egos. What we have found is these practices help us focus our energies on reconditioning our behavior and making choices that bring serenity rather than chaos into our lives.

Provoking the Pattern

1. Ego announces its presence through emotion and/or physiological changes. When you feel yourself becoming angry, for example, you may also notice a clenching of your jaw or tightness in your chest. These tactile signals indicate your ego is exerting its control. When you become aware of these signals, you have the opportunity to intervene and decide how you want to proceed. By provoking the pattern you disrupt mindless, patterned behavior, act with intention and make a conscious choice.

Practice: Intentionally set out to do one or two things differently over a period of time. This might be as simple as responding with patience when you are delayed; replying gently when someone is angry; cracking a joke when you feel like screaming. Shake things up a little and discover it is your choice!

2. When we begin to *clean the attic* we find a number of myths in our guidance system. At times, a specific incident or pattern of behavior gets in our way and we are compelled to look at the belief system that got us there. Proactively, we can check for pre-conceptions in our guidance system as an ongoing, lifelong process.

Practice: Over the next thirty days, look at ways you sabotage your own wellbeing.

For example, if you accept an invitation to a social engagement when you are stressed by other obligations — consider the belief that propelled you to accept. A need to please? A concern about rejection? The loss of social standing?

The Cosmic Irony

Once we begin this journey, we discover the *great cosmic irony* is we already possess a truly integrated, functional and perfect guidance system. We don't need external programming. Our belief systems are at best intellectually interesting distractions and at worst, outright deceptions. As reflections of Source energy, we are perfect in our manifestations. We are goodness and love! Wouldn't it be wonderful if we were confident enough to let our higher self, our own energetic force for goodness and love, light our way?

The Source created a world based on order, balance and harmony; we are a part of that creation and already perfect. Although we may have lost conscious touch with the Source, we can begin to condition ourselves for this experience. Begin today by becoming aware of your guidance system. Like this Chapter's poem, give some thought to the superficial bonds that make you the daytime you that you are not — come out of the dark!

CHAPTER THREE |
TAMING THE EGO – AN ODYSSEY

Two people have been living inside you all your life.
One is the ego, garrulous, demanding, hysterical, calculating,
and the other is the hidden spiritual being, whose still voice
of wisdom you have only rarely heard or attended to. [12]
— Sogyal Rinpoche

There's something wonderfully calming and restorative about syncing an Apple iPhone with a Microsoft PC, creating a sense of integrated, perfect order. What would life be like if we could sync up our day-to-day experiences with our true nature, our *hidden spiritual being*?

Carl Jung said, ". . . as far as we can discern, the sole purpose of existence is to kindle a light in the darkness of being." [13] Why is it we continue to operate in the dark, out of sync with our true selves? Once we begin to understand the belief and guidance systems that propelled us into adulthood, what keeps us from kindling this light?

Meet the governor, our ego. Like the mechanism on an eighteen-wheeler that keeps it from careening down a hill, our ego governs our feelings, emotions, expectations and sense of self. Our words and actions then affirm or challenge the ego. As Rinpoche suggests, the ego can be *garrulous*, *demanding*, *hysterical*, and *calculating*. To be sure, the ego does not like to be challenged.

We are about to begin an uncharted odyssey to tame the ego — uncharted, as we each have unique, unpredictable egos. To "kindle a light in the darkness of being" will require patience, practice and the willingness to let go of the lifelines we have created for ourselves — the limitations, expectations, labels, judgments, attachments and patterns that have defined us. When we begin to tame the ego, we begin to let go of who we think we are and discover who we are. This part of the trek is not easy. The ego is a formidable opponent — but the results are life changing!

A Clinical View

Before we begin this leg of our journey, let's step back to the 20th century when Dr. Jung distinguished himself as one of the eminent explorers of the human psyche. A student, protégé and colleague of famed psychiatrist Sigmund Freud, Jung's concepts eventually moved beyond Freud's clinical theories. Fascinated by the mysteries of the mind, Jung's work was enhanced by his spiritual and mystical approach to understanding human behavior.

Essentially, Jung describes the mind as consisting of three theoretical constructs:

1. The Conscious;
2. The Personal Unconscious; and
3. The Collective Unconscious.

According to Jung, the ego governs the *conscious* mind. It acts as the driver or manager of all our conscious activities. The *personal unconscious* is thought to be the repository of conscious experiences that, for some reason, became repressed and/or separated from the conscious mind but could be brought to consciousness with reasonable ease. Jung saw the *collective unconscious* as a gateway to the higher self. He saw this as our psychic inheritance, the reservoir of our collective experiences as a species, our connection to the eternal.

Although Jung described the ego as determined to control everything and place significant roadblocks in the path of integrated awareness, he believed the goal of life is to realize the higher self transcends all opposing influences of the conscious and unconscious. Jung envisioned a state-of-being where we are neither individual nor the whole of creation, but perfectly balanced in a new center, closer to all people, all life and the universe itself.[14]

Much Ado About Ego

Spanning eastern and western religions, crossing socio-economic, cultural, ethnic and philosophical differences, ego is recognized as a common nemesis to achieving order, balance and harmony.

Like the mind, ego is a theoretical construct — ethereal, elusive and uniquely customized by each person's experiences, thoughts, actions and reflections. As you might imagine, opinions vary as to the role and importance of the ego. Is the ego capable of allowing new information from our true self to the same degree it is inclined to elevate our false self? Subject to volition, does the ego participate in the pursuit of higher consciousness? And, we wonder, since the ego is a conceptual construct, do these theoretical attributes really matter?

Without attempting to bridge the philosophical chasms between clinical scientists, behaviorists and transcendentalists, there appears to be common agreement the phenomenon of the ego must be addressed.

The problem of life is to overcome the basic human disability of egoism.

—Aldous Huxley

Blessed are the meek, for they shall inherit the earth.

—Jesus, Sermon on the Mount

It helps to regularly undo the hard-won ego development, to unravel the self and culture you have woven over the years. The night sea journey takes you back to your primordial self, not the heroic self that burns out and falls to judgment, but to your original self, yourself as a sea of possibility, your greater and deeper being.

—Thomas Moore, Dark Nights of the Soul

The primary function of the ego is to keep you from knowing your higher self.

—Wayne Dyer, Your Sacred Self

An essential part of the awakening is the recognition of the unawakened you, the ego as it thinks, speaks, and acts, as well as the recognition of the collectively conditioned mental processes that perpetuate the unawakened state.

—Eckhart Tolle, A New Earth

Untamed, the ego continues to operate on beliefs and guidance systems we have unconsciously maintained and embraced. Unaware, it's like relying on *Cliff Notes*[15] about our lives before we've had the chance to enjoy the fullness of our own experience.

Viewpoints vary as to how one goes about taming the ego. Yet, ancient and contemporary philosophers agree taming the ego is essential to living with greater awareness and waking up to our true self. Because ego's insidious nature often obscures the fact that it is a theoretical construct — subject to influence by discipline and choice — the first challenge is to become aware of how the ego has been functioning.

It is within this conceptual framework that we begin to explore the tenacious and intractable ego and its influence on our spiritual evolution.

Conditioning for Conscious Awareness

One of the most common signs of ego at work is our 'knee jerk reaction;' that spontaneous emotional impulse that causes us to respond in a way that reflects our past emotional reaction to similar circumstances. How 'past' might take us back to the cradle! If we want to attain conscious awareness, we need to tame or recondition the ego. As we tame the ego, we free ourselves from the constraints, burdens and distortions of guidance systems operating below our radar screen.

Let's examine some of the characteristics of ego and look at ways to increase our conscious awareness — improve our ability to recognize when ego is driving our experiences. Let's coin this process *egonition*!

1. Distractions and Diversions

Ego abhors *nothingness*. Carlos Castañeda's teacher, Don Juan Matus, explained a sorcerer, one who lives by the Source, is empty inside.[16] This emptiness describes a state of mind both conscious and meditative where the external influences so easily grasped by the ego are subdued to allow our inner-self complete access to our consciousness. To the ego, nothingness is a state of weakness — impoverished the ego has nothing to work with!

When we meditate or try to silence our busy minds, we experience how rapidly the ego rushes in to disrupt the stillness. Like white blood cells rushing to the site of an infection, ego attempts to fill the empty, quiet spaces with distractions and diversions — from the ordinary to the fantastical — keeping us in ego's stronghold. Entertaining and immediate, we tend to be easily seduced by ego's more charming nature and forget about our intended journey.

Without doubt, patience is an essential element of our *egonition* tool kit. Although the ego has an impeccable, albeit slanted, long-term memory, its childlike short attention span is a handicap. With time and repetition, we are able to wear the ego down and recondition it, as we become more awake and aware. Once we begin reconditioning our ego, we will find our true selves showing up in ways that surprise and delight us!

2. Limitations and Expectations

Ultimate Reality cannot be limited by any name or concept.

—3rd Guideline[17]

Ultimate Reality, our true self, knows no boundaries and imposes no conditions on our awareness, abilities, talents and intellect. Limitations and expectations emanate from the ego side of consciousness and almost always have the effect of restricting our potential for wholeness.

Self-imposed and, more pointedly, self-described, we learn about limitations very early in our lives, coming fast and furious in a society that encourages competition. *I'm not good at math. I can't play baseball; I'm always the last one chosen.* Sound familiar? The specifics will be different for every individual, but the impact is nonetheless profound as our ego builds a false sense of identity, a fabrication of self.

We understand the physical limitations that cause us to choose one path over another, but keep in mind the individuals who beat the odds — football players with small builds, skiers with one leg, blind painters, deaf musicians. With some exceptions, limitations are based on unexamined, rote beliefs that distract us from achieving our highest potential. In many cases, we impose these beliefs by common clichés we attach to our self-image: *Are we defined by our anger? Impossibly burdened by jealousy? Hopelessly destined to be a workaholic? Are we without any power to change because that's just the way we are?* Is it time to rewrite the scripts?

If the limitations we choose to define ourselves do not contribute to order, balance and harmony, they are ego driven and it's time to release these limitations and open up possibilities!

Expectations present a bigger set of challenges. There are two broad categories of expectations — those we establish for ourselves and those we impose on others. The expectations we establish for ourselves might include constructive guidelines to achieving a greater connection to Source energy. To avoid confusion, let's call these *disciplines*. One of the essential ordering principles of life is discipline and, without it, our journey toward higher awareness will be all but impossible. Whether it takes the form of meditation, ego awareness or a commitment to discover our spiritual self, discipline is required. In part, discipline is the catalyst that compromises the ego and enables a new conditioning of our psyche — inviting conscious choice.

The second category is expectations we project on others. Ego-driven, expectations projected outward are the precursor to disappointment. They establish a path that puts another person's actions or reactions in a box and cuts us off from the power of intentionality. Do you see the difference between *I would like* and *you should*? This distinction sounds elementary, but one phrase is intentional and the other phrase is limiting. We either create an environment that liberates our counterpart to act in his or her own way with intentionality, or we establish defined lines of expected behavior or response. Expectations get even more counterproductive when they are unspoken. How often have we felt hurt or offended because someone did not read *our* mind or follow *our* script?

George Bernard Shaw once said, "Our lives are shaped not as much by our experience as by our expectations."[18]

We have all experienced the white water of limitations and expectations; this whorl can devastate the best-laid plans. There we go again, thinking we can plan our way to happiness. What if we paid attention and began to challenge each and every limitation and expectation? How would it be if we said, *sorry ego, I'm just not buying that story anymore*?

How would life be if we began to discover that ego has this all wrong?

3. Labels and Judgment

I had tried so hard to please that I never realized no one was watching.[19]

—Mark Nepo

Nepo's quote strikes a universal chord, as most of us have struggled to affirm ourselves through others — wanting to distinguish ourselves as worthy of love and connection. As part of the human condition, many of us share the common experiences of not feeling lovable enough, being a misfit and sensing we are alone in this world. We know these fears are imbedded in our belief systems at a very young age; yet, they continue to keep us off balance, out of harmony.

The conundrum here is although we want to feel love and connection — our desire to *distinguish* ourselves as worthy of love and connection is the very thing that keeps us from experiencing love and connection! It keeps us separate.

Consider what happens when we set up a yardstick to label or judge others; this same yardstick then applies to our self. This leads to highly subjective, often unreasonable comparisons between our self and others; and because no one else is watching, we end up trying to prove our self against these metrics, not realizing others have their own unique yardstick for labeling and judging.

As you might imagine, labeling is a favorite tactic of the ego — quickly dispensing words and opinions that reinforce our feelings of superiority, inferiority and separateness. Distinguishing ourselves from others is one of ego's favorite methods of pitting us against 'the competition,' keeping us separate — an unlovable misfit, all alone in this world!

When we judge, our self or others, our ego-driven opinions of right or wrong, good or bad, moral or immoral are equally swift and immediate. Like labeling, judging also separates us from others and diverts us from getting to know our true nature, our spiritual essence — discovering we are a loveable, fully integrated spirit with a connection to all living things.

> As long as the human condition is experienced as separate from Ultimate Reality it is subject to ignorance, illusion, weakness and suffering.
>
> —7th Guideline[20]

4. Attachments

The ego loves attachments — these are ego's toys and playthings. A sucker for life's dramas, the accoutrements of both success and failure, the ego has not been conditioned to nurture our higher selves. As a result, it's easy to attach ourselves to careers, houses, possessions, vacation trips and the psychological attachments of self-importance, entitlement, victimization and hopelessness. And, it seems, we willingly allow ourselves to be defined by what we do, what we have and how we compare to others.

Make no mistake, the rich and famous are not necessarily the standard bearers of ego-induced behavior. Notably, ego's attachment to poverty, victimization and hopelessness is as equally compelling and limiting as its attachment to wealth, self-importance and power.

Whether our attachments are to possessions, status, or the myriad of other psychological hooks, these addictions are promoted by the ego and have nothing to do with who we are. Do we really want to be defined by our job, self-pity or the composition of our countertops? Is this enough?

5. Patterns

If you always do what you've always done, you'll always get what you've always got.

—Unknown

How easy it is to repeat the same stimuli and evoke the same responses! How does ego reinforce these patterns of behavior? Why do we continue to respond the same way to the same stimuli and expect a different outcome?

Let's take a look at some common patterns:

a. Choose partners who are emotionally unavailable
b. Wait until the last moment to meet our commitments
c. Choose jobs based on convenience or security rather than interest
d. Ignore obvious intuitive or visual signs a new relationship is looking like the old one
e. Seek physical and/or sexual contact before connecting emotionally, intellectually or spiritually

We all experience some patterns in our lives. These reinforced behaviors are pay dirt for our ego. How easy it is to get caught up in the same experience over and over again!

The Five-Year Itch

[*The Seven Year Itch* is an iconic 1955 movie based on a theory that marriages lose their luster by the 7th year.]

I've already shared with you that I was nineteen and pregnant when I married my high school sweetheart. Two years after our second child was born, I found myself in a marriage where we had little in common. My husband was a sports fanatic, someone who loved to play and watch hockey, baseball, football, basketball, soccer — anything with a puck or a ball. I wanted to discuss books, politics and current events; share poetry; explore ideas; and occasionally attend a stage play or concert.

What surprised me was the degree of my agitation and discomfort, which seemed far beyond the pale of not sharing similar interests. The physical manifestations were incredibly strong. In fact, during this time of high stress, I developed phlebitis and a pulmonary embolism. After two weeks in the hospital, I returned home to the same sense of agitation and discomfort. I asked for a divorce. We had been married five years.

Two years later, I married a man who loved to read, discuss books, politics and current events. He read poetry to me on our first date and shared my interest in the arts. We moved to the country, subscribed to 'Organic Gardening,' built a compost pile, put in an organic garden, harvested and canned vegetables for the coming winter. We had a child after two years and life seemed perfect until I began to feel the agitation and discomfort. I decided he wasn't ambitious enough and providentially, discovered he had been unfaithful. It seemed like permission to walk away. We had been married five years.

Three years later, I married a man who was highly ambitious. At age twenty-eight, he was the vice president of

*a major highway construction company and worked 10
to 12 hours per day. He was well traveled, loved to read,
discuss books, politics and current events. He didn't
understand poetry, but shared my interest in performing and visual arts. He had a son from his first marriage and neither of us wanted to have more children.
Life seemed idyllic. We had a large home near a lake,
great jobs, good income, good health, bright children
and many friends. Right before our fifth anniversary, I
began to feel the agitation and discomfort. I instigated
arguments and pointed out our differences. He was not
easily persuaded and challenged my thinking.*

*Was this a pattern? I was five when my father died,
when my first love left me. Of course, my ego was operating from a well-practiced pattern of fear and flight
after five years. It was my first conscious effort at taming my ego. My third marriage lasted another 10 years.*

—Kathleen

We all have patterns waiting to ambush our quiet contentment or sense of self. Imagine what life would be like if we
intervened before ego theatrics sent us spiraling into some
new melodrama — if we acted with conscious intentionality
in co-creating our lives.

The Practice of Egonition

We know ego is manic about keeping us in high drama,
creating all manner of distractions and diversions. When
we begin to feel a sense of bliss, or a moment of serenity,
ego might use fear or shame to suggest we are unworthy
of pleasure — or engage pride to appeal to our vanity and

sense of separateness. Ego is the usual suspect for prompting feelings of shame or entitlement — both are spiritually disabling, causing us to think we are not connected to a greater whole, that we are separate. Sometimes it feels as if we are slammed by ego-charged emotions. At other times, ego sneaks through the back door with a niggling question like *who do you think you are?*

More dramatically, our ego influences major decisions like jobs or relationships. Perhaps you, or someone you know, clung to a job or relationship that created so much misery it began to affect his or her health. We've met a number of highly skilled, intelligent people who report they stayed in a job or a relationship because they felt trapped by some impoverished 'life under the bridge' story of being homeless, unloved and unwanted. Rationally, no one had life experiences to cause a concern about this fate. Yet, ego was feeding an old, fictional and universal fear. To wake up from our fabricated dream state and begin living a conscious life, we first need to recognize when ego is at the helm.

No doubt, confronting the ego is a continuing, life-long challenge. In Paulo Coelho's book, *The Witch of Portobello*[21], the main character Athena is counseled by her teacher Edda to "reprogram your self every minute of each day with thoughts that make you grow," suggesting Athena "laugh at the absurdity of her doubts and anxieties."

As we become more aware of the ways in which our ego, our self-appointed governor, tries to derail us, we realize the *absurdity* of letting this thoughtless maniac drive our decision-making. The ego expects us to give in easily, as we've done for decades. If we stop and consciously challenge ego, or remain patiently observant without acting, the ego loses its power and force. Over time, we begin to realize ego is more illusory than substantive. More frighteningly, we sometimes discover we have been operating on automatic pilot and the pilot is only five years old! Do you want to continue on this flight path or are you ready to make a change?

Consider the effects of *Ego vs. Source*:

Fear vs. Love
Anxiety vs. Serenity
Envy vs. Affirmation
Pity vs. Compassion
Entitlement vs. Humility
Separateness vs. Oneness
Self-Centeredness vs. Other-Centeredness
Self-Loathing vs. Self-Love
Competitiveness vs. Collaboration
Self-Consciousness vs. One Consciousness
Chaos vs. Clarity
Biased vs. Open and Expansive
Stereotyping vs. Individual Gift Recognition
Sameness vs. Otherness

As an example, observe the difference between pity and compassion:

Spencer, an eight-year old girl, and her Grandma Kate were watching the TV show, 'America's Got Talent.' The program was early in the audition stage and four older women were dressed in 1950s prom dresses singing rock and roll songs from that era. All had bouffant hairdos and heavy makeup that, in Kate's opinion, only served to highlight their wrinkles, weight and questionable performance skills. When the act was over, Kate was about to express pity when Spencer turned to her exclaiming, 'Aren't they beautiful in their pretty dresses and fancy hairdos?'

Compassion isn't limited to caring for those who are less able or less well; unlike pity, compassion also means the absence of criticism and judgment for those who choose playful expression and act with unabashed good nature, spontaneity and all the variations that make us wonderfully different!

Life is a journey from hypocrisy to sincerity, from self-centeredness to other-centeredness and love, from self-deception, ignorance, and illusion to self-honesty, clarity, and truth. We are all immersed in these struggles whether we realize and accept them or not. Even if we reject them, we have made a choice. [22]

—Wayne Teasdale

A Light from Within

Are you ready to dismantle the automatic pilot feature and make the transition from living at ordinary levels of consciousness to living beyond the ordinary?

To live beyond the ordinary requires we live our lives with intentionality. And, intentionality requires we become acutely aware of the ways in which our ego and egoist patterns of behavior retard our growth and interfere with our ability to co-create a life of order, balance and harmony. This awareness, more than anything else, will help us recondition or tame our ego. When we no longer operate from fear, doubt, suspicion, distrust and a negative self-image, we will find our self connected to the Source — a repository of love, respect, honor, integrity and impeccable truth. Here, now, this moment, we begin "to kindle the light in the darkness of being."

"First we take Manhattan then we take Berlin!" Leonard Cohen's proclamation for personal power is a drum roll to begin active vigilance of egoist behavior. We know ego announces its presence in a variety of ways. Physically, we may become aware of a tightening in our solar plexus, elevated blood pressure or other signs of stress. Extreme emotional reactions — sudden anger, impulses to lash out or shut down — are almost always ego-based.

These physical and emotional signals are part of our internal radar system, designed to alert us ego is attempting to seize the moment, our moment! It is here, at this critical juncture, when we have the opportunity to begin taming our irascible ego by making a conscious choice and acting with volition. If we stop and challenge the underlying feeling(s) and wait for an alternative, it will come. There are rarely moments or circumstances that do not offer us choices. It's the difference between living life with intentionality or tumbling down that rabbit hole once again.

Recently, we met a woman who suffers from profound insecurity and a negative self-image. She lost her husband several years ago and continues to hold on to that loss, struggling daily with her pain and defining herself by her widowhood. She says she wants to move on, but when encouraged to meet new people or attend social events, she is quick to point out what she does not like about the new people or events. Fueling her self-imposed isolation and pain, she seems locked in the prison of her own ego. The kindliness of friends and family may help strengthen her resolve; however, it requires her active vigilance and volition to co-create another way of being.

When we act with volition, we act with conscious awareness. When we begin practicing this self-awareness, we begin to experience Jung's vision of an integrated awareness — where we are neither individual nor the whole of creation, but perfectly balanced in a new center, closer to all people, all life and the universe itself.

The Cosmic Giggle

Laughter is the closest distance between two people!
—Victor Borges

Once we've begun to challenge and tame the ego, we are often tickled by its duplicity and hilarity. Sometimes, the beast is best tamed by learning to laugh at our self.

In *A New Earth*, Eckhart Tolle said, "When you observe ego in yourself, you are beginning to go beyond it. Don't take the ego too seriously. When you detect egoic behavior in yourself, smile. At times you may even laugh."

The cosmic giggle brings to light the irresistibly funny, ironic notion of a lifetime spent tangling with a theoretical construct called *ego*. Intended to help us understand and explain our behavior, we've spent most of our life being resigned to or resisting ego's distorted view of our true selves. Sometimes life is stranger than fiction! Are you ready to provoke the pattern?

Provoking the Pattern

Because the ego announces its presence through emotion and/or physiological changes, we can use this internal radar system to intervene and decide how we want to proceed. By provoking the pattern, we have an opportunity to disrupt mindless behavior, act with intention and make a conscious choice.

1. Self-Labeling

Practice: Listen to yourself. Pay attention to the language you use to describe yourself. Do you reflect your authentic self or is your description ego's rote response? For example:

a.) *Unconscious* Description: *I am so stupid when it comes to computers.*

b.) *Authentic* Description: *I have avoided learning about computers because I am:*
   (i) *not interested in this technology,*
   (ii) *intimidated by technology,*
   (iii) *have other priorities in my life, or*
   (iv) *waiting until they design something that is more intuitive.*

The unconscious descriptions label and reinforce limitations. The authentic descriptions are statements of fact about the circumstances without a need to label or limit one's potential. Each time you find yourself labeling yourself or others, rewrite your script using authentic and compassionate language.

2. Self-Imposed Limitations

Practice: Observe yourself. Pay attention to the choices you make.

For example:

a.) *Imposed* Limitation: I'm too old/fat/set-in-my-ways (fill in the blank) to travel to foreign countries/dance/ find a mate (fill in the blank).

b.) *Without* Limitation: I am open to all the joy, wonder, love the universe has to offer. If I choose not to travel/dance/find a mate (fill in the blank), this choice will not be based on self-imposed limitations. The decision will be based on conscious choice.

Each time you find yourself making a decision based on a self-imposed limitation, use the *Practice of Inquiry* discussed in Chapter Two:

1. Why do I believe this is true?
2. Is it a self-imposed expectation about reality?
3. How does this expectation limit me, or my options?
4. What would my life be like if I did not hold this expectation?

Through the Looking Glass

We said this would not be easy. For most of our lives we've relied on our well-honed egos to guide us — automating our routine thoughts, actions and decisions. In our fast-paced world, the idea of acting with conscious volition seems to threaten our energetic bandwidth. Before we reach this conclusion, let's take a look beyond the ordinary.

In Lewis Carroll's *Through the Looking Glass*, a sequel to *Alice in Wonderland*, Alice engages in a game of chess where the pieces on the chessboard come to life. Sometimes our lives seem like a game of chess — powerless, subject to the influence of external and impersonal forces. In many cases, we go through the motions but miss the experience. Is this easier? Does less conscious awareness require less energy?

If we stop to consider these questions, each of us would acknowledge the incalculable cost of unconscious living

— economically, spiritually, energetically and emotionally. Within our own microcosmic lives, when we avoid an internal or external conflict, work assignment or commitment, we soon realize the energetic cost of avoidance is far greater than the energetic cost of conscious vigilance and volition. At the macrocosmic level, it is clear our unconscious living is wreaking havoc on our communities and planet.

Because so much of our time is spent multi-tasking through a complex barrage of information — high-traffic and high drama — we may trick ourselves into thinking that conscious volition takes more energy. And, since so much of our life experience is condensed in our mind, our ego has all the raw material it needs to further entangle us in its fictional web.

How much raw material? Scientific studies seeking to determine how many thoughts we process in a day report averages ranging from 12,000 to over 70,000.[23] This rate works out to between 8 and 50 thoughts per minute, an immense load of information to process! Fortunately, there is ample scientific evidence that we have the power to significantly reduce this traffic and focus our thoughts — with the added benefit of lowering our heart rates, breath rates and blood pressure.

The capacity of the human mind to reason, react, envision, imagine, intuit and inspire is far beyond our imagination. With 100 billion neurons, the brain is truly a miraculous and mysterious organ, still challenging clinicians and scientists to understand its exotic, intricate nature. When we add to this the complexity of the conscious and unconscious mind, the mystery gets even more enigmatic!

It is in the context of these expansive resources that we begin — with vigilance and volition — to tame the ego and embrace the Source.

CHAPTER FOUR |
DO TWO HALVES MAKE A WHOLE?
THE COMPLETION MYTH

Let there be spaces in your togetherness,
and let the winds of the heavens dance between you.
—Kahlil Gibran

Isn't it curious, with all the possibilities and potential for wholeness, ego-driven theatre continues to captivate us — especially when the drama includes romance? We spend years constructing a false self, an identity fabricated by the ego. Then, when we take our fictionalized self to market — to mate with someone else's fictionalized self — we expect to find someone to complete us. Do two fictionalized selves make a whole?

In *The Secret Life of Walter Mitty*[24], we meet a man who spends his days dreaming about a more exciting life, one filled with heroic adventure, fame and fortune. This story has worldwide appeal as we each have a secret life. And, because we have a phenomenal capacity for inventiveness, we wonder how many of our tens of thousands of thoughts per day are devoted to romantic fantasies. For some of us, these fantasies are a healthy way to ease our minds, soothe our souls or escape from the sometimes-hard realities of life.

Prisoners of war and other captives have survived by virtue of this magnificent quality to transport their selves mentally, emotionally and spiritually. Although some of us tend to be more romantic than others, we each experience these flights of fancy and imagine a better, more exciting world for ourselves.

If we accept the premise that most weaknesses are over-extended strengths, it is not surprising that *over-romanticizing* our lives leads to disappointment, disillusionment and frustration. We know many of our belief systems were formed before we had conscious awareness. We also recognize many of these beliefs are based on social myths. If we compound this information with our tendency to create romantic fantasies, we begin to understand the complexity and treachery of looking for another person to make us whole. Yet, we continue to hear people announce they have found their 'soul mate,' discovered their 'other half' or 'been made whole.' Is this even possible? What happens when we rely on someone else to make us whole?

Lost in the State of Euphoria

The notion of finding someone to 'complete us' dates back to the earliest biblical times and religious tenets that suggest when two people marry they become one. What does this 'one' look like, act like? Do we merge intellectually, spiritually, physically and emotionally? If we become one, what parts do we keep and what parts do we discard and who, exactly, is in charge of this process? The irony is we rely on the other person to perfect what is already perfect. The casualty is we suspend our own, unique evolutionary power when we look to someone else to make us whole.

Admittedly, there is nothing more intoxicating than romance. Who among us has not or would not enjoy the feelings of excitement and passion that accompany this experience? This newly discovered sense of love, connection and redemption seems to lift us from ordinary levels of consciousness; everything seems brighter, more distinct, more alive! A natural aphrodisiac, we lose ourselves in a state of euphoria. Literally, we lose ourselves. What's more, even if we know we are lost, we don't care. What's important is we have found someone who meets our needs, satisfies our hunger and engages our passion. During this period of intoxication, we may feel completed.

Most of us have been lost in romantic illusion; hopelessly addicted, many continue to seek this illusion over and over again.

The Good Son

When I was young, I believed what I was told, and to some extent what I saw, but not necessarily what I felt. I remember being told, 'you shouldn't feel that way,' as if I was getting it all wrong. Unlike Kathleen, I was a compliant child and learned to deny or suppress my feelings — focusing on doing those things that gained acceptance and avoiding those things that brought disapproval.

It wasn't until my late thirties, while trying to preserve my first marriage, when a therapist asked me to describe my feelings. I replied, 'Do what? I haven't the slightest idea what you are talking about.' I buried my feelings for so many years I didn't know what I felt, or more sadly, how to feel. I spent almost forty years becoming the son my parents envisioned or the husband my first wife envisioned. What happened?

In my case, the notion I needed someone to 'complete me' began early in life. I grew up in a traditional family where the roles and responsibilities of a man and woman were well defined. From an early age, I was told I would meet someone, fall in love and we would have our own home and children. I never considered the possibility or value of experiencing life as an individual. The patterns and pre-programming were very effective. This was not some sinister plot by my parents. They were simply passing on what they had been taught — a norm for pursuing life.

By the time I was 18, I was a packaged, branded product. Inside the box you would find the model of a proper young man — armed with principals of character, concepts of duty and responsibility. I would attend college and prepare to become a husband, father, good provider — the head of a household. I was ready and anxious to be made whole by the union of marriage. And I did just that. I kept this branding alive through two marriages, six children and a few career changes, not giving any attention to who I was, what I felt or cared about.

My memories are no less sweet because I took this prescribed path; however, at age 58, I finally gave attention to the stirrings of my own awakening. I began again by discarding the completion myth. What craziness to think someone else will make me whole!

—Bonner

Today, there are still tribal, cultural and religious customs where children are matched and mated without the child's consent. Although this custom appears in conflict with western nation ideals of freewill and individual rights, arranged marriages were practiced by the upper class in Europe until the twentieth century. In third-world nations, this custom continues to be openly practiced, involving girls as young as eight. In other parts of the world, including the United States, arranged marriages still occur within certain ethnic and religious communities.

In most developed countries, societal norms have shifted in the past forty years, placing less emphasis on early marriage, in favor of individuals pursuing an education and career. Still, finding a partner continues to be enormously important to both men and women. With the career-life balance tipping toward later marriages and childbirth, the biological clock often mounts the pressure to marry, and not the prospective grandparents.

Despite the shifting societal norms, the idea that one of the purposes of partnering is to find someone who completes us, makes up for our deficiencies, is still alive and well.

We aren't suggesting that marrying or partnering is wrong. Pragmatically, mating or insemination is essential to the continuation of our species. The idea we want someone who will nurture and enrich our life is both desirable and understandable. The concept we *need* someone to make us whole is flawed. The completion myth is based on the idea that someone else is necessary to make us whole, by providing emotional, psychological or spiritual elements we think we lack and are incapable of, or unworthy of, developing for ourselves.

Exposing the Myth

Depending upon another to validate that we are worthy of love gives that person control over our emotions and our self-esteem. We have given up our power.[25]*
—The Buddha in Your Mirror

The belief that we need someone to 'complete us' presupposes we are not complete. If we don't feel whole, we are destined to struggle through life with a sense we are inadequate and unworthy. Who among us has not experienced these feelings? Some indeed may have matured with a powerful and uncompromised sense of self, but for most of us, life is a constant search for someone or something to fill the empty space inside us and help us feel worthy and complete.

In *Looking for Mr. Goodbar*, a 1977 film starring Diane Keaton, a young teacher begins her search for the perfect man, *Mr. Goodbar*. Her desperation to fill her emptiness leads to bar hopping, sexually promiscuous behavior, drugs and unstable men. Unlike Walter Mitty who fantasizes his exploits, the protagonist in *Mr. Goodbar* engages in self-destructive behavior as a means of finding more excitement and meaning in her life. Although this pattern of behavior may seem extreme, most of us know someone who has demonstrated this level of desperation.

Why do we expect another fragile soul to fill our emptiness? Do we underestimate our own divine power or do we imbue others with exceptional power?

When we look at nature, the natural balance of creation, we see that it has provided everything we need to sustain life on earth. Why then would we assume that creation failed to provide everything we need to function as a healthy,

62   DO TWO HALVES MAKE A WHOLE? THE COMPLETION MYTH

self-aware, evolving being? If we have the air, the sun, the life-giving energy to live physically on this earth, why would we not have the capacity to experience our wholeness in relationship to others?

Discussion

Kathleen: *Becoming whole seems to be a lifelong, if not infinite pursuit. If we wait until we're whole to enter a relationship, most of us would be single. With this in mind, what might we consider — commit to — when we engage in relationships while we are still ego-driven and operating from our fabricated, false sense of self?*

Bonner: *The idea of being incomplete is a philosophical perspective. If I think I am incomplete or need someone to make me whole, my self-identity gets bound up in the relationship and I rely on my partner for my sense of well-being. We know where that leads!*

Kathleen: *What about soul mates? Many people believe they've found their soul mate — someone who completes them.*

Bonner: *I think we're all soul mates. When I hear this, I suspect it's more about discovering a physical, intellectual, spiritual or emotional connection that attracts them to one another. No one else can 'complete me, make me whole.' That's my job!*

Kathleen: *Yet, we have both been in relationships where we expected to find completion. What important lessons have you learned through your relationships that guide you now?*

Bonner: *There are many — but here are three that come to mind:*

1. *Do not enter a relationship expecting your partner to change or conform to your image or fantasy of a 'perfect partner.'*
2. *Lovingly support and nurture the growth of your partner. If your focus is on what you expect, it is coming from a place of self-centeredness and not love.*
3. *Commit to discovering your true self; act with awareness, integrity and authenticity. This means acting from love and not a need for affirmation or validation.*

How about your lessons learned?

Kathleen: *It seems we've learned many of the same lessons. Let me add a few.*

4. *Consider your partner a spiritual muse with whom to practice unconditional love, acceptance, forgiveness and gratitude.*
5. *Do not take yourself, your partner, or your relationship too seriously. Embrace humor, irony and irreverence. We are, after all, bundles of energy and light.*
6. *Allow for openness, authenticity and creative expression in all you do; avoid judging, labeling, shaming and blaming.*

Letting Go

Intellectually and intuitively, we know the path to wholeness comes from within. However, it is our longing to fill our emptiness that compels us to look outside of ourselves to partners, careers, homes and possessions to fill this void. In the process, we often lose ourselves to these attachments. In Chapter Three we looked at our attachment to things; here we consider what happens when we become attached to others. Both are ego-driven.

When we attach our self to others, we seek affirmation and validation; the consequences are predictable. How many of us have spent far too much time and energy on someone who is not interested in us? Otherwise normal, well-adjusted men and women obsess about an unrequited love by incessant checking of email, voice mail, driving by their home, frequenting favorite restaurants, waiting for their calls, spending sleepless nights wondering what they could do to change reality. As bizarre as this sounds, many of us have spent untold hours trying to change what is. This is the high cost of ego. When we attach ourselves to others, whether or not they reciprocate our feelings, we ignore our own divine light in favor of attracting and pleasing someone else.

This doesn't mean we stop caring about others or enjoying the experience of giving and receiving pleasure. It means we stop expecting others to make us feel whole. It is the only way we free ourselves to evolve. In a partnership, allowing the other to be who they are is the only way to support and nurture one another's growth.

When we let go of the idea we need someone else to feel whole, we discover our capacity to manifest love and find beauty in new ways of being in a relationship. There are many times in our lives when we love and cherish someone who, for whatever reasons, is following a different trajectory in life. The reality is we do not need to partner with everyone we love. Love has no boundaries or limits; it expresses itself in ways we can only just imagine. When we begin to explore our wholeness, we free our self to generously love, support and celebrate others in exploring their wholeness with or without us.

What if we took all the energy we consume trying to manage, alter or change a potential partner, or change reality, and directed this energy toward discovering our own wholeness? What if we then had the experience of connecting to someone who was aware of his or her own wholeness? Imagine the freedom and liberation of exploring life as an adventure in change rather than looking for someone to fill an empty space. Are you ready for an intentional relationship?

Rethinking Relationships

When the sense of euphoria evaporates, as it will, we are faced with the reality and rigors of living as a couple: working, creating a home, paying bills and planning for a better future. Somehow, feelings born of spontaneity and romantic attraction drift away — vanishing in the routine of life.

Is there a way to maintain this romantic illusion? Do we even want to? What if there is a better way of being in a relationship — one where both feel empowered and whole? What if the only requirement is for each person to be more of who they are?

We know the mystery of relationship often defies reason and understanding. We learn by experience — our own and through others. As we, Kathleen and Bonner, considered our collective body of relationship experience — with what we learned in the research, writing and rethinking for this book — we began to fully appreciate the powerful effect of intention in forming healthy relationships. It is from this frame of reference that we invite you to consider other ways of being in relationships.

The Third Entity

In 1923, Austrian born philosopher, Martin Buber, wrote an essay, *Ich und Du*, which means 'I and Thou.' In this work, Buber claims there cannot be an *I-You* relationship, as there is no true exchange between self and *other than self* until there is a self to relate to. Buber is referring to our true, divine selves and not our fabricated ego selves. Until we begin to present our true selves and dismiss our fabricated selves, our partnerships will be powered by egos in an artificial bubble of togetherness that is fragile, requires enormous energy to maintain and must be continuously re-inflated.

As we discussed, it doesn't make sense to wait until we are fully evolved to enter a relationship. If we did, it might signal the end of our species! To avoid this catastrophic fate, there are other saner ways of being in a relationship before we realize our true selves.

A number of philosophers have described a relationship as being comprised of three entities: (1) You (2) Me and (3) WE. Rather than becoming one, this precept acknowledges the individual nature of two people who create a third relation-ship entity — the WE. The WE requires care and nurtur-ing by the You and Me. Here, the individuals do not become 'one;' they build and create a relationship as a foundation for their partnering.

From his poem, *The Third Body*, Robert Bly offers a poetic description:

> They obey a third body that they share in common.
> They have made a promise to love that body.

Age may come, parting may come, death will come!
A man and a woman sit near each other;
As they breathe they feed someone we do not know,
Someone we know of, whom we have never seen.

Because we evolve differently and change over time, the idea of building and creating a third entity to support a relationship offers us an opportunity to connect with one another while freeing us to explore our individual wholeness. All three of these entities require separateness and togetherness. If any one of the three entities of You, Me or WE, gets lost or absorbed by the other, the relationship invariably breaks down. The maintenance of these co-existing entities relies on the energy of intention to ensure the integrity of the individuals and the solidarity of the structure to promote the health, wellbeing and sovereignty of all three entities.

Essential to co-creating and sustaining intentional relationships is each person's *individual* pilgrimage to discover the perfection of his or her wholeness and divine nature, setting the stage for being in relationships without losing one's self or power.

Singing Myself

I celebrate myself, and sing myself,
And what I assume you shall assume
For every atom belonging to me as good belongs to you.
                    —Walt Whitman, from Song of Myself

When we discover our own sense of perfection and completeness, we activate and enable our true self to be known and appreciated. We become a tower of light and some will be drawn to that light and some will not. When we act from our own sense of wholeness, those who accept us are the people we will choose to explore relationship with. Not for the purpose of completion, but for the purpose of complementing one another's experience. In Mark Nepo's words:

> . . . singing the song of who we are, is one of the surest ways to refind our place. It is how we wake from pain, from sleep, from apathy and doubt. So even when confused and somewhat in the dark, take the risk to voice yourself and the map of the world will come into view. Sing who you are, even if you don't know, and your deeper instinct to relate will show you the way.[26]

Rethinking Commitment

When we, Kathleen and Bonner, are out together, people have made the assumption we are a couple, sometimes inquiring about our relationship. Although our personal relationship has many dimensions, changing over time, it thrives because we have learned from experience that connection is more powerful than commitment. For us, relationship *is* the manifestation of connection; considerations about commitment are less important. We are all infinitely connected to one another and if we share this path with one another for a time, or a lifetime, it is our choice to manifest love or not. A promise by one or both does not alter this reality. Our own experiment in relating has liberated both of us to more freely and exuberantly open ourselves to the *why not* of living in these bio-suits and inspired our collaboration on this book to share our journey.

The conventional wisdom of our time promotes the notion that the joining of two individuals is best achieved by commitment. A commitment is a promise; more specifically it is a pledge to do something in the future or accept an obligation to promote a particular cause or action. How often have you heard someone complain, *he or she won't commit*, as though this is the acid test for a loving and successful partnership? We wave commitment across the couple like a magic wand and expect miracles.

According to recent statistics, over 50% of all first marriages end in divorce in the United States; this increases to 67% for second marriages; and 74% for third marriages with an upward trend. When you combine this information with statistics that suggest nearly 60% of married women and 50% of married men say they don't plan to leave their partner but would never marry them if given that choice today, it paints a rather dismal picture of committed relationships.[27]

What happens in marriage that causes people to shut down? We believe there are two motivating, underlying factors:

1. The disappointment of one or both partners when they discover the other person does not make them feel whole; and,
2. The discovered false sense of security that commitment is enough to hold two people together for a lifetime.

By contrast, the concept of connection suggests a level of intimacy that is individually liberating and produces an environment for coherence and continuity. In our, Kathleen's and Bonner's, individual experiences, and through the experiences of others, we find when two people bond and recognize a mutual connection based on one or more aspects of their physical, emotional, intellectual or spiritual bodies (four aspects of connection), there is a powerful, symbiotic interest in nurturing and growing a relationship.

Let's consider the difference between connection and commitment. The experience of connection does not presuppose the nature of the relationship; a commitment does. When we share a connection, the bond is to a common purpose, the growth and nurturing of one another — liberating us to share a pilgrimage of experiences. The focus is on living life to the fullest; there is openness to what will evolve. When focus is only on commitment, there is a structure and expectation of how this will evolve. Often, both partners relax into the false security of commitment, expecting the status quo. To them, commitment is the end game; they have already arrived.

Certainly, we need to make an initial commitment in time and attention to explore and promote the four aspects of connection. In this respect, the commitment is to open oneself to the possibility of connection. It is then when we are able to determine if we have the connections, and the maturity, to nurture and support a relationship.

This in no way implies that committed relationships and marriages are unimportant or don't succeed. Instead, it suggests that rather than *relying* on commitment, we set our intention on promoting the growth and nurturing of one another; on bonding through connection; on exploring life as an adventure in change; and adapting to the endless possibilities that exist in the bright light of Source energy.

Perfection

Each individual must fill his own niche in exquisite time and eternity.

—Mary Baker Eddy

By now we know when we are challenged with self-doubt, we have allowed ego to take the lead. When we live our lives from awareness and authenticity, we recognize our perfection.

In this lifelong, infinite pilgrimage of self-discovery, we need to continually challenge our beliefs, debunk myths, tame the ego, act with intention and stay in the moment through awareness and authenticity. We know this requires constant vigilance, but the results are remarkable. When we discover our own perfection, we no longer look for someone else to make us whole; we look for someone with whom we connect. When we connect with the knowledge of our own evolving perfection, we discover there is no end to this surging life force; we are limitless in our ability to co-create our lives!

Provoking the Pattern

1. Self-Assessment: Sometimes it is hard to see our self. Most of us are afflicted with a case of 'true-self' blindness because we have operated for so long from our ego-driven identity. In this assessment, we want you to claim your otherness by identifying those aspects of your self that make you unique.

Practice: Make a list of 20 characteristics that distinguish your incomparable otherness. Do not edit as you go. If you become stuck, send an SOS to a friend for help. You might be surprised!

2. When we look for a partner to make us whole, we doubt our own worth and fail to see our own perfection. Recall, ego announces its presence through emotion and/or physiological changes. When you feel self-doubt, you may experience

a shortness of breath, a sinking feeling in the heart or solar plexus or tightness in your chest. When you are aware of these signals, you have the opportunity to intervene and decide how you want to proceed.

Practice: Pay attention when you feel the physiological sensations of self-doubt — when you find yourself feeling intimidated by or 'less-than' your companion(s). To disrupt this mindless, patterned behavior, make a conscious choice to breathe deeply and remind yourself of your own perfection. Consciously manifest love for your self and your companion(s). Recall, we are all fragile and flawed. No one has power over us unless we allow someone to have power over us. If you are ever in fear of harm, listen! This is not ego, it is our natural ability to sense danger and protect our self.

An Optical Delusion

> *A human being is part of the whole, called by us 'universe' – a part limited in time and space. He experiences himself, his thoughts and feelings as something separated from the rest – a kind of optical delusion of his consciousness.*

> —Albert Einstein

Due to this "optical delusion" of separateness, we humans have a tendency to take ourselves far too seriously. Compounding this, when we embark on a journey of self-discovery, we tend to get a little pious about our pilgrimage. When we lose our sense of humor and sense of perspective it's a clear sign ego is operating at full tilt!

As we liberate our self and retool our guidance system, the ego will perceive the body satellite careening through the universe. Fear sets in. It's up to us to face this fear with humor and love, recognizing both our oneness and otherness.

We invite you to take a moment to breathe deeply and find your cosmic giggle. We are about to venture into The Great Liberation. Are you ready to discard some of your old beliefs about the prescribed path, let go of the completion myth and discover new ways of living life and being in relationships?

CHAPTER FIVE | **THE GREAT LIBERATION**

Come to the edge
We can't we are afraid
Come to the edge
We can't, we will fall
Come to the edge
They came
And he pushed them
And they flew!
— Guillaume Apollinaire

Sometimes we need a push to break away from the insecurity of our fabricated self and experience our own exquisite power. Why does insecurity have such a hold? Are we afraid of achieving our highest potential? So it seems.

The following quote by Marianne Williamson has been attributed to Nelson Mandela to the extent it has become an urban legend; its enlightened plea an anthem for humankind to challenge these fears, to liberate our self and others:

> Our deepest fear is not that we are inadequate. Our deepest fear is that we are powerful beyond measure. It is our light, not our darkness, that most frightens us. We ask ourselves, who am I to be brilliant, gorgeous, talented, fabulous? Actually, who are you

not to be? You are a child of God. Your playing small does not serve the world. There is nothing enlightening about shrinking so that other people won't feel unsure around you. We were born to make manifest the glory of God that is within us. It is not just in some of us; it is in everyone. As we let our own light shine, we unconsciously give other people permission to do the same. As we are liberated from our own fear, our presence automatically liberates others.[28]

As we continue to explore ways to rekindle our light, we keep in mind this journey is both thrilling and frightening. For too long, we have been condensing life into thought. Rather than living awake and aware, with intentionality, we have found comfort and solace in intellectualizing, dramatizing and *awfulizing* — based on a lifetime of well-rehearsed, ego-driven scripts. The familiarity of these scripts binds us to mediocrity, repeating the same stories over and over again. When we give up these scripts, we get scared. Are you ready for that push off the edge?

Beyond Fear

Whether you think you can or can't, you are right.

—Henry Ford

Why is it we feel discontented, constantly looking for diversions or excitement, ways to fill the void, objects or people to make us whole? Is it fear? If so, what are we afraid of: failure or success, rejection or acceptance, judgment or obscurity? Are we afraid of finding or not finding a partner? What about the fear of aging: wrinkles, physical infirmaries, mental incompetence, death? Do we worry about reaching the end of our lives without a sense of purpose?

What might it look like if we got beyond our fear? Have you ever experienced the liberation of doing something so pure, invigorating and natural, you felt transformed? If so, you realize what it's like to act from love, where nothing holds us back and causes us to second-guess ourselves. These are the times when we jump off the proverbial edge, knowing we are connected to the Source.

Discussion

Bonner: *Let's talk about why we call this chapter 'The Great Liberation.'*

Kathleen: *One of my deepest fears is I am powerful beyond measure. In the first four chapters we looked at where we are and how we got here. What we haven't faced yet is why we deliberately hide behind our self-imposed or other-imposed 'norms.' Are we afraid to rekindle our own light? What would life be like if we unshackle ourselves from our ego fear and experience what must be The Great Liberation?*

Bonner: *Since fear is a defining emotion for many of us, what do you see as the antidote of fear?*

Kathleen: *Before we talk about antidotes, it's important to distinguish between 'being in fear' and 'detecting danger.' We are equipped with an innate radar system to detect danger, which signals our flight or fight response to avoid harm. We must pay attention to these signals.*

But, 'being in fear' is a mental and emotional habit that immobilizes us, keeps us from expanding our boundaries, exploring the world or otherwise moving forward with decisive, love-based action. To me, love is the antidote of fear. When I act from love, I am not afraid —I have courage to move toward truth.

Bonner: *How does being in fear affect our outlook and actions?*

Kathleen: *In fear, we are ridiculously myopic. In fact, I sometimes entertain myself by replaying fear-based reactions in my mind because they are so 'cloak and dagger' fantastical! Fear takes us out of the moment and pulls us into a swirling vortex of anxiety fueled by imagination — radically diminishing or disguising our options and sabotaging our efforts to co-create our lives.*

Bonner: *You sometimes refer to Divine Intelligence. Is there a Master Plan?*

Kathleen: *Divine Intelligence is interchangeable with the Source, God, Spirit, Ultimate Reality – all terms used to express the spiritual essence of one's true nature. Part of this essence involves an individuated volitional power to co-create our lives. If there is a Master Plan, I'm sure it includes this creative power to influence the quality of our experience. As we said earlier, whether we access Source power or not, we are all co-creating our experience every day.*

Bonner: *What catalyst moved you toward your personal liberation?*

Kathleen: *I've had many small awakenings in my life. These moments have led me inexorably —albeit slowly, incrementally —to liberation. For most of us, The Great Liberation is gained over many years and opportunities to free ourselves of self-imposed and other-imposed burdens. My most dramatic liberation occurred about* six years ago. In this chapter's story box, *The Outlier*, I share experiences that highlight the profound healing power of the universe.

Bonner: *Are you willing to share more of the fears you wrestle?*

Kathleen: *I mentioned my mother-lode fear of being powerful beyond measure. Another life-long struggle is my fear of emotional intimacy. As you know, I had the pleasure of sitting with a Buddhist-trained spiritual leader in a number of satsangs and individual sessions over a one-year period. During one of our individual sessions, he suggested my relationship with you was being lived out in my head. I laughed so hard I cried and immediately asked you to examine this with me. Of course, he was right. I, like so many others, 'live out' relationships in my head, imagining the truth. My fiction was telling myself my male partners were afraid of intimacy — not me. What I discovered was my own fear kept me from opening up. I was 'protecting' my heart by all the thoughty[29] mind-driven exchanges necessary to perpetuate this fairy tale. As you know, I am much better at living 'out loud' these days, risking intimacy.*

What about the fears you wrestle?

Bonner: *I began my spiritual journey so late that one of my greatest fears is I won't have time to fully explore life awake and aware. Of course this makes no sense when I consider my infinite, timeless nature. Writing this book looms as a new fear! I continue to scare myself each time I sit down to compose, edit or critique our collective work; I am infected by self doubt and ask myself who am I to presume I have something worthy to say?*

Ah, my ego. Each time I jump off this cliff, contribute my work and realize I didn't crash land, I'm liberated to take the next step and the next.

Bonner: *Having known you for some time now, I think one of your strengths is your awareness. What role does awareness play in gaining a sense of liberation?*

Kathleen: *In my growing awareness, I can no longer ignore myself, play small or hide behind the many fabricated stories about who I am. I struggled with this at first because I quite enjoy my fanciful and imaginative head-trips, my refuge in many storms. What I'm discovering is once we become aware, it's very hard to pretend. Authenticity is the liberator.*

Bonner: *If we co-create our reality, can we co-create our liberty?*

Kathleen: *I think we reclaim our liberty. Letting go of our fear and insecurities helps us rediscover our authenticity and connection to the Source.*

Bonner: *We've talked about the 'perfection' of humankind while at the same time suggesting each of us is 'flawed and fragile.' How do you reconcile these two observations?*

Kathleen: *I think we are perfectly imperfect! Our spiritual self — our oneness with the Source, God, Allah — is perfect. And, because we have the volitional power to co-create our lives, we make choices. If we give up our volitional power to ego-driven drama and fear, we experience life as flawed and fragile beings. If we choose to access Source power and manifest love, we move toward order, balance and harmony. Both outcomes depend on choices we make. As evolutionary beings, both lead to new experiences and awareness.*

Thought leaders have long recognized the power of overcoming fear and uncertainty as a way to liberate our self, to reach our highest potential.

In his first inaugural address in 1933, President Franklin D. Roosevelt spoke of the Great Depression and rallied the nation by saying, "We have nothing to fear but fear itself." He understood a country paralyzed by fear would not be able to pull itself up. Through this awareness, he helped mobilize a nation.

In his book *Power vs. Force: The Hidden Determinants of Human Behavior*, David R. Hawkins, M.D., Ph.D. discusses the influence of fear on wellness and the disease process, stating:

> In spontaneous recovery, there's frequently a marked increase in the capacity to love and the awareness of love as a healing factor. . . . Recovery from any disease process is dependent on willingness to explore new ways of looking at one's self and life, which includes the capacity to endure inner fears when belief systems are shaken.[30]

What if we moved beyond our fear and tapped into the Source? How would this change our perspective, our experience, our capacity to reach our highest potential? Is it enough to think we can?

The Outlier

About nine years ago, I woke up with a horrible pain in my shoulder after playing three rounds of golf that weekend. Within a few days, the pain became worse and migrated to both my wrists and hands. After a number of visits to different specialists and a series of diagnostics, I was referred to a Rheumatologist who diagnosed my condition as Rheumatoid Arthritis (RA). By the time I was seen, I had lost significant flexibility in my wrists and strength in my hands. It took both hands for me to turn the key in my ignition or turn a standard doorknob. I used a side-body push to open swinging doors. I was exhausted most of the time and my business travel became a hardship. My body seemed to be collapsing in on its self. We tried many different pharmaceuticals, including steroids. Nothing seemed to help.

Three months later, on my way home from work, I could almost taste the bitterness and dread of getting home and having to turn off the ignition and open the back door. I felt victimized, succumbing to pain and fear. Just then, I caught my eyes in the rear view mirror and saw a fragile, crippled woman I did not recognize. From a place deep within my being, I said, 'Screw this! I am NOT a victim and I am NOT going to live in fear.' After this, I took charge of my care and began to assert my power, connecting to the Source and banishing fear. The results were almost immediate. My Rheumatologist is still baffled, unable to explain why I continue to test positive for RA but have no symptoms of this unforgiving disease. He tells me to continue doing whatever I am doing.

During a trip to New York with two friends, we walked 7 to 10 miles per day, reminiscing about our friendships. One, a medical doctor, has known me for almost 30 years. She said she always has a hard time describing me to her professional colleagues. When I asked why, she said I am what they call 'an outlier' — someone who recovers from progressive, chronic, disabling diseases and rebounds from surgeries without any scientific medical explanation. She tells her colleagues it's as if I am able to heal myself.

Does this reflect my capacity to endure inner fears when belief systems are shaken? Did my willingness and determination to explore new ways of looking at my self and my life contribute to my changed reality? Is this one of the mysteries, or are we able to access the Source to co-create our experience and heal our self?

—Kathleen

Once we begin to recondition the ego, discard our fabricated self and access the Source, we will no longer be able to play small and pretend. This is the cost of awareness. When we liberate ourselves from fear, we take on the prodigious responsibility of achieving our highest potential.

To be sure, our highest potential does not equate to a singular purpose. We know many people who have been frustrated by the popular myth of 'finding one's purpose' — discovering a vocation, avocation or public service specifically intended for their life on Earth. Although some people think they have found their purpose, we believe each of us is capable of multi-purposes and achievements far beyond our ego-limited imagination. Some of us may choose to specialize in one area of work or service; however, many of us are generalists with a wide range of interests, abilities and knowledge. In our exploration, we find job satisfaction has more to do with the love we manifest in our work than the work itself. Whether you earn your living as a rock star or stonemason, what you do is not who you are.

As one consciousness, we believe all knowledge that was or ever will be exists within us all. When we begin to access Source power and co-create our lives through intention, we open ourselves to the higher vibration levels of Divine Intelligence, pure consciousness and pure love. It is then when we discover we are powerful beyond measure and any perceived limitations were solely of our making.

The Unpossessed

> *Many of us lust after some possession, only to feel a nagging emptiness once we attain it. We try to ignore this emptiness, thinking that the next object will somehow fill us. But it never does.*[31]

> —Wayne Teasdale

Many first nation, indigenous people saw themselves as *inhabitants* of the world rather than *inheritors*. The fundamental difference between these two concepts is far reaching — affecting the development of social and cultural structures over the past 10,000 years. Ownership of real, intellectual or artistic property and other possessions may create civil order; however, the possession of property has also been the source of wars, mayhem and crime. In our discussion of liberation from possessions, it is not to undo centuries of property law, but to free ourselves from our *attachment* to property and possessions.

When Janis Joplin sang, ". . . freedom's just another word for nothing left to lose," she suggested a seminal truth that freedom requires we liberate ourselves from our attachment to possessions. This is not to propose we take a vow of poverty to attain spiritual awareness; property and possessions are an integral part of our society. But, rather, to consider how our attachment to property and possessions has the effect of holding us hostage to living life at ordinary levels of consciousness.

Throughout history, there are a number of references to ancient people who considered themselves stewards of nature's abundance and cultural treasures. Stewardship is about taking care of entrusted gifts. Although indigenous people receive more attribution for their sense of being inhabitants rather than inheritors of the Earth, many religions teach the importance of stewardship in protecting our precious resources.

Embracing the idea of stewardship rather than ownership is a liberating experience. For many of us, money, possessions and the trappings that accompany wealth or poverty[32] somehow begin to define our life and misdirect our energy. Then, when we attempt to build relationships around the accumulation or absence of stuff, we learn very quickly the cost, energy and attention to material things does not produce the desired results. Financial stress is typically one of the top three reasons offered for the dissolution of relationships. The other two are sexual relations and family relations. Isn't it odd financial stress is right up there with the more complex, contentious human aspects of relating?

In the movie *Fight Club*, the character Tyler Durden, played by Brad Pitt, says to Cornelius, played by Edward Norton, "What you own ends up owning you." Beyond the financial burden, beyond the occupied space, beyond the maintenance and repairs, beyond the insurable risks, there is a cost when our self-image or self-worth is appropriated to our ownership status.

When we let go of our attachment to possessions, we change our mindset. We are no longer defined by what we own, where we live, or the composition of our kitchen counters. We begin to choose well and act as stewards. When we make this shift, we begin to liberate ourselves from unhealthy attachments — become more attuned to who we are, what we want in our lives, and consciously decide how much energy we are willing to give inanimate objects. With this awareness, we will no longer appropriate our self-image to stuff. Imagine the sense of liberation. It's like losing thousands of pounds!

Losing the Joneses

One of the more pathological aspects of attachment to possessions is the mythological practice of keeping up with the Joneses. Driven by ego's effort to encourage competition, many of us have had the experience of striving to attain possessions and improve our status or social standing. Some who are taming their egos say the risk here is almost like checking out of 'life' as we know it!

A Progeny Story
Falling Apart or Falling in Place?[33]

Taming the ego is equivalent to checking out of life — at least the life I lived before I became aware of my ego. The jolt from blindly operating through the ego to more consciously making choices has had an immediate and profound impact on my life.

Early in my efforts, there were times when making choices without the support of my ego felt like a unique form of depression. In spite of feelings of happiness, gratitude and joy, I began to sense I had little in common with people I had interacted with for years. Conversations about new things, bragging about our kids, competing on the tennis courts or speculating on recent gossip held little appeal. I no longer cared about keeping up with the 'Joneses,' managing a team at work or maintaining a string of engagements on my social calendar.

The best analogy to describe the internal change of taming my ego is moving a car from the fast lane to the slow lane while driving down a highway. Although the car is still moving at about the same speed, I enjoy the journey instead of trying to stay ahead of traffic, as if I was competing for a pole-car position at the Indy!

This change has not been easy. Taming the ego takes a lot of work and effort. On a daily basis I remind myself (via 'self talk') of my true essence versus my ego. Looking back over the years, it is when I listened to my ego that I traveled down the wrong path, got myself into trouble or landed in situations that provided no joy or satisfaction. Letting go of the ego has also led to moments when I thought my life was falling apart, but soon realized it was falling in place. These outcomes may not have been what I envisioned or intended at the time, but I'm sure they are what my true self wanted and needed all along. I am just now beginning to experience a sense of liberation.

—Kirsten McLean

Losing the Joneses is liberating, and as Kirsten suggests, it also signals a transition to a different way of being in the world, of connecting with others and choosing how we spend our time and energy. The transition is sometimes unsettling; however, we find the resiliency of spirit and power of love helps us create favorable conditions to retain old friendships and connections in our growing awareness.

Good Vibrations

The Beach Boys sang about 'good vibrations,' and we have all had the sensation of what we might describe as positive or negative energy. This experience can be as simple as walking into a funeral home and feeling the energy of grief or sitting in the bleachers while fans explode with cheers when the hometown team hits the winning run. We feel these vibrations in our self when we are depressed or excited. Like a battery, we talk about feeling energized or depleted.

In Chapter One we observed that the cosmos, including the intricate realms of the sub-atomic world, consists of energy. We are *bundles of energy* and we resonate energetically with one another and our environment. Over the years, there has been significant research by scientists, clinicians, alternative therapists and environmentalists who look at the effects of energetic force on behavior, health, and the habitability of this planet. In more recent history, studies have also included the effect of technology on the planet and the life it supports.

As reported in his book *Power vs. Force*, Dr. Hawkins' interest in this subject was inspired by a number of awakenings in his youth, including a near death experience that led to what he described as:

> . . . a transformation of such enormity had taken place that I was struck dumb with awe. The person

I had been no longer existed. There was no personal self or ego left — just an Infinite Presence of such unlimited power that it was all that was.[34]

In his studies, Dr. Hawkins explored the energetic influence of different levels of behavior and awareness. Using the science of kinesiology,[35] he developed a method to measure the energetic levels of spiritual evolution. For example, he attributes an energy level of 20 to feelings of Shame, 100 to Fear, 250 to Neutrality, 500 to Love and 700–1000 to Enlightenment — with each new 'awareness' resonating at higher vibration levels. Dr. Hawkins supports this fascinating study by scientific validation; however, he captures many of his findings in the following simple quote:

> We are life. It's a scientific fact that 'what is good for you is good for me.' Simple kindness to one's self and all that lives is the most transformational force of all.[36]

Our life force is the energetic projection of who we are. The more we embrace and promote our true selves in our actions and dealings with others, the more our vibrating energy aligns with the Source. Who we are and how we project ourselves becomes synchronized. This is harmony.

Embracing Our Oneness

> *Disciplined practice is essential to the spiritual life; yet spiritual attainment is not the result of one's own efforts, but the result of the experience of oneness (unity) with Ultimate Reality.*

> —8th Guideline[37]

Once we begin to see beyond the ego version of self, we move to the edge and glimpse the reflection of Ultimate Reality and light. This recognition of our oneness with all living things allows us to surrender, unafraid, to our true self. This is the experience Apollinaire describes in his poem. When we come to the edge, we prepare ourselves for flight to a higher vibratory level and expression of self. We are one with the Source. Here, we discover our power and beauty is the manifestation of our love and not the mastery of our work.

"Is there a way to explain the purpose of hawks gracing the sky with perfect pirouettes; the softness of a cat in quiet repose; or the timbre of aspen leaves chiming the wind?"[38] When we embrace our oneness, we embrace the love, splendor and mystical expansiveness of the universe. We are not alone because we are not separate.

> . . . what transforms us is not what we do but our inte-
> gration with what is. What we do in the way of our
> spiritual effort, our habits of prayer, meditation, com-
> passion, and love are all important; but the cause of
> change is the inner mystical process of union with the
> source. That, and that alone, is what brings about inner
> change and carries us into the everlasting roots of our
> expanded identity with the divine.[39]
>
> —Wayne Teasdale

Celebrating Our Otherness

Celebrating our otherness may seem alien to the concept of oneness. However, there is a clear distinction between uniqueness and separateness. The perfection and beauty of the universe is found in its infinite expression of nature. Consider the seemingly endless varieties of plant and animal life, the earth's topography and geothermic activity, all the shapes, sounds and images in a world teaming with millions of life forms — and, we humans, all different in attitudes, opinions, shapes, sizes, skills! Our uniqueness doesn't mean we are separate. It means we are perfect in our otherness.

Rather than trying to change our companions to be more like us, or more like our perception of how they should be, consider how relationships would be if we embraced one another's otherness. This does not mean we welcome every person's action, inaction or comments. We will still need agreements to sustain and manage households and agreed upon ways to resolve conflict. It does, however, mean we honor *otherness* as a gift and quit the insanity of trying to change one another. Friends of ours, married for over 50 years, attribute their successful partnership to retaining their otherness, with the wife stating, "There was no way I wanted him looking in the mirror and seeing me!"

When we embrace our oneness and celebrate our otherness, we liberate our self from the very scary prospect of trying to remake our self or our partner based on our ego-driven, fabricated sense of the perfect mate. Hallelujah!

Love Is Not a Commodity

When we quit treating one another like projects, we may begin to appreciate one another's life force. Both of us have been in relationships that seemed to demand reciprocity as a condition for tenderness, support, sexual connection and, it seemed, love.

Many otherwise mature adults act as if love is a commodity to be bargained for, offered or withheld. If we haven't personally experienced it, we likely have friends who treat love as a commodity — setting up conditions for the relationship. I will love you, make love to you, treat you with kindness, if you (fill in the blank): take the high-paying job, buy me a new (house, car, jewelry, boat, motorcycle), take me on this trip, stop going out with your friends, get a (haircut, shave, lose weight, work out), pick up your socks, cook dinner, etc.

As we listen to friends who have signed up for Match.Com, eHarmony or other dating services, the conditions seem even more specific and dogmatic. We know people who ruled out a potential match because of facial hair, style of clothing or eyeglass frames. Perhaps love has become a commodity! People are shopping for potential mates by leafing through catalogs — smiling faces of mostly good, kind people — who provide a 'profile' of who they are and what they want in a mate. Although this method has proved to be a good way to meet people who share interests and values, there seems to be a greater opportunity and temptation to select potential mates based on superficially ascribed commercial values.

When we treat love as a commodity we are likely acting out of fear — fear of intimacy, fear of giving too much or not getting enough, fear of making the wrong choice in partners, fear of not getting the love we want and need. When we stop treating love like a commodity and move beyond our fears, we find we create the conditions that allow love to be experienced.

Who's Keeping Score?

In many partnerships, there is a tendency to 'keep score' in an effort to make sure both partners are making equal contributions to the relationship. When both partners engage in this scorekeeping, it is a set up for ongoing conflict and disappointment. We have heard young parents say things like *I've had the kids three nights in a row, it's your turn* or *I've (fill in the blank), it's your turn*. With two working partners and the stress of job and family, this kind of scorekeeping is understandable. Yet, when we keep score — scrutinize our loved-one's behavior, judge his/her performance and demand reciprocity — we put an additional burden on an already stressed relationship. When we keep score we are hiding behind a fear. Are we afraid we will give more than we get? If so, is it worth the cost in time, energy and its impact on the relationship? What if we communicated with love rather than bargaining with carrots and sticks? What if we simply asked our partner to take the kids because we need a break?

Consider how this might look if we put down the carrots and sticks and liberated ourselves from trying to manage relationships on the basis of reciprocity and duty. Imagine how our relationships might be if we opened ourselves to a free-flowing, unencumbered exchange between two perfectly unique individuals learning to manifest love for the mutual benefit of one another. Why not?

An Eye for an Eye

> *If we practice an eye for an eye and a tooth for a tooth, soon the whole world will be blind and toothless.*
> —Mahatma Gandhi

Gandhi's message about the futility of 'getting even' is a testament to the futility of non-forgiveness and the liberation of acceptance.

When we carry resentment against someone, the implication is we are exacting an eye for an eye and a tooth for a tooth. In this ego-driven revenge drama, the non-forgiver generates negative energy and breeds stress-induced toxins. The un-forgiven may experience a sense of loss or confusion, but in cases where s/he is no longer in contact with the non-forgiver, s/he escapes the influence of this drama.

Why then do we hold grudges? Recall our ego encourages behaviors to keep up the fiction we are separate, entitled, inviolable or unworthy. What about that mythological sweet revenge? In our experience, the ego finds revenge sweet for a nanosecond then wants us to extract more, feeding the resentment and fueling the negative energy. When we tame the ego, and act with conscious awareness, we understand resentment is not only toxic to our emotional, physical and spiritual bodies, but also negatively impacts all those who come within our energetic field.

As we move toward living with greater awareness, our perspectives change to match our evolving reality. In Don Miguel Ruiz's book *The Four Agreements*, he tells us, "Nothing others do is because of you. What others say and do is a projection of their own reality, their own dream."

Shifting our perspective from the 'offenses of others,' we are less likely to experience resentment. When we feel resentment, we have an opportunity to practice forgiveness — a conscious, volitional act that helps us maintain emotional integrity and spiritual health.

Wayne Teasdale offers:

> The spiritual journey only begins in earnest when we no longer experience the need to judge others, when we begin to take responsibility for our own inner development.[40]

What would life be like if we were more accepting of one another? Would we learn to appreciate one another's unique qualities without judgment? Is acceptance of one another's differences essential to our own spiritual evolution? We think so. When we accept and forgive one another, we express our compassion for the beauty of both our oneness and otherness. We may not *forget* the events, the indiscretions or breaches, but our willingness to accept and forgive also strengthens our resolve to let our own light shine.[41]

When we open our heart to acceptance and forgiveness, we liberate ourselves from petty grievances, grudges and resentments — we get out of our way!

The Runaway

I was in my early thirties with three beautiful children, a loving husband and a successful career in labor relations at General Motors. We lived in a lake neighborhood with good friends and enjoyed an active social life. By all outward appearances, I was happy. If asked, I would have said 'life could not be better!' Why then, did I want to escape?

My job was a twenty-minute commute along a nondescript highway south of Flint, Michigan. On my way home from work, I would often fantasize about passing my exit and not turning back. In fact, there were a number of times when I was ten miles past my exit before I realized I had not made the turn! Did I think I would find liberation by running away? What was this all about?

I had forgotten about these forays until my daughter told me there have been times when she thought about picking up her kids from school and driving until she

*reaches one of the coasts with the idea she will spend
the rest of her life on the beach. She said, 'the craziness
of such thinking is I don't like beaches — the desire to
run away seems less crazy!'*

*Why do we engage in these fantasies? Is this our way
of coping with the pressures of life or could it be our
true essence stirring to be liberated from the collection
of attachments, patterns, expectations, possessions and
mindless routines that seem to be the collage of life in
our thirties and forties?*

*What I find liberating is the realization that these feel-
ings are likely normal, healthy signals we need to give
attention to what is important in our lives. I have no
doubt others, perhaps more rebellious or desperate,
keep on driving, leaving behind family and friends, only
to discover there is no way to escape from one's self.
Liberation seems to have little to do with where we live.*

—Kathleen

Provoking the Pattern

1. *Quell the Fear*: By now, most of us know the physiological
and psychological signs of fear. We are not talking about our
innate radar system to detect danger. Here, we are talking
about the ego-driven fear that immobilizes us from expanding our boundaries, exploring the world or otherwise moving
forward with decisive, love-based action. When we are able
to move beyond fear, we liberate ourselves to achieve our
highest potential and create conditions for healing, creativity and spiritual growth.

Practice: Pay attention to the physiological and psychological signs of fear. Each time you recognize one of these

sensations, breathe deeply and think or speak the words *quell the fear* or *all is well*. Consider the belief system or guidance system that led you to believe you were not competent enough, good enough or smart enough. Consider Marianne Williamson's plea to let your light shine and liberate yourself from fear. Keep practicing.

2. *Stay Soft in the Heart and Soft in the Belly*: More often than not, when we are in conflict or negotiating for something we want or need, our ego tees us up for battle. Kass Atkinson, a very wise therapist in Santa Fe, New Mexico, advises her clients to "stay soft in the heart and soft in the belly." Creating this condition reduces tension and helps us open up as one human being to another. When this happens, the energy shifts and we find ourselves connecting to the person(s) on the 'other side of the table,' experiencing oneness.

Practice: The next time, and every time, you find yourself nervous, tense or worried about conflict, simply remind yourself to stay soft in the heart and soft in the belly. Make it your mantra. It works!

The Great Guffaw

> *Life is too important to be taken seriously.*
>
> —Oscar Wilde

Some of us grew up reading or listening to stories from the *Reader's Digest* magazine section *Laughter is the Best Medicine*. Featuring reader contributions about humor in their daily lives, these stories helped us shift our perspective and find comfort in poking fun at ourselves. Over the years several studies and our own experience demonstrate the positive correlation between laughter, health and healing. Yet, we spend an enormous amount of emotional energy navigating the minutia of daily life — traffic, lost socks, missing keys, cancelled flights, renegade technology! And, it seems, our ego has an enormous appetite for misappropriating energy.

Talk about co-creating our reality! If we examine our life — the events and circumstances, the twists and turns, the serendipities and disappointments — we can either find the humor or feel the weight. The choice is ours.

Letting go of things that oppress us, instill fear in us or paralyze us from acting liberates us to achieve our highest potential as sentient beings. Life's challenges and adversities do not define us or reflect our worth; we are separate and apart from our experiences. As author James David Audlin said, "Even when you experience adversity, it will be understood not as an assault on you, but simply as a part of the story."[42]

The more we let go of things that oppress us — by confronting fear, dismissing anxiety or simply stepping back and viewing them as part of the story — the more we will smile and laugh at the psycho-dramas we weave. Drawing on the irrepressible energy of the Source, the great guffaw dispels any imagined weight and opens us to endless possibilities.

Oscar Wilde is correct, "Life is too important to be taken seriously."

Love Is a State of Being

Spirituality isn't child's play. My sentences will tear to pieces anyone who listens to them. After all, what you awaken to is the truth, which shatters the illusion of who you've believed yourself to be.

—Nisargadatta Maharaj

Zen Buddhism refers to enlightenment as 'The Great Death;' put in other words, enlightenment is 'The Great Liberation.' When we let go of our ego-defined selves and get out of our way, we are able to access the Source — God, Atman, Allah, Buddha, Intention, Spirit — and rediscover our true selves. Still, shattering the illusion of who we are isn't child's play. We need maturity, experience and motivation to let go of our fabricated selves.

For most of us, shattering the illusion of who we believe we are occurs over many years, decades, a lifetime. To do so is the ultimate liberation of our tortured, fictional selves. As we awaken to our true selves, we begin to let go of fear and discover we are love.

In *The Power of Now*, Eckhart Tolle writes:

> Love is a state of being. . . . You can then feel the same life deep within every other human and every other creature. You look beyond the veil of form and separation. This is the realization of oneness. This is love.[43]

Consider the implications. We do not give or receive love. We manifest love.

PART TWO |
CO-CREATING OUR WAY

CHAPTER SIX | **THE EDGE WALKERS**

The universe is transformation;
our life is what our thoughts make it.
—Marcus Aurelius, Roman Emperor 161–180

Whoosh — now that we've been pushed off the proverbial edge, we know our liberation from fear means we have to give up the beliefs, patterns, practices and perceptions that keep us from achieving our highest potential.

In the first five chapters we discussed the importance of *getting out of our way* — to reconnect to our true nature and act with awareness. Now we'll explore ways to gain confidence in our ability to act with intention — transforming our self and our experiences. Powered by Source energy, we will see how intention interacts seamlessly with our true self and coexists with volition. Then, as we consciously co-create our way, we begin to affirm our self and others.

In his pastoral comedy, *As You Like It*, William Shakespeare wrote:

> All the world's a stage, and all the men and women merely players: they have their exits and entrances; and one man in his time plays many parts. . . .

We, of course, agree. Life is often the purest form of theater. As we transform ourselves, we soon realize we are also producer and director. Most of us abdicated these roles, letting phantom, unchallenged beliefs propel the continuing drama. When we accept our role as producer and director, we act with volition and intention — co-creating our experiences and our relationships. As Emperor Marcus Aurelius said in the second century, "our life is what our thoughts make it."

And, our thoughts change! As we become more aware and discover new information, our reality shifts — or does it?

An Ode to Copernicus

> *Do not be conformed to this world, but be transformed by the renewing of your minds.*
> —Romans 12:2

In 1543 just before his death, Nicolaus Copernicus published his definitive work proposing Earth was not the center of the Universe. This heretical proposal was further aggravated by his proposition the Earth *orbited* the Sun!

Less than one hundred years later, Galileo Galilei pursued and verified Copernicus' views through astronomical observations. As a result, Galileo was arrested and, during the Catholic Inquisition of 1632, convicted of being *vehemently suspect of heresy* because his *views were contrary to scripture*. Forced to recant his findings, Galileo, considered by many as the *Father of Modern Science*, spent the remainder of his life under house arrest.[44]

The lens of cognition and volition alters our perception of the world around us. Throughout recorded history, humankind has created and abandoned myths in response to new knowledge and actions in response to this knowledge. Sometimes the response is slow in coming. The Catholic Church did not formally recognize Copernicus' finding that the Earth is not the center of the Universe until 1992 — 450 years later! In a Vatican paper, Pope John Paul II declared the ruling against Galileo was a ". . . tragic mutual incomprehension."[45] If you find this stunning, consider a recent poll report that one out of five people *still* believe the Sun revolves around the Earth;[46] and almost one in ten believe Elvis is still alive![47]

The message seems clear — just because we confront a misconception with facts doesn't mean others will change their opinions. For example, statistics suggest shark attacks in the summer almost never cause death and we are more likely to die from furniture falling on us.[48] Yet, most of us spend our fear on possible shark attacks. Why is this?

Neurologically, when we take in information, we process it through a part of our brain called the hippocampus. As we think about what we've learned, we form ideas and beliefs, which are routed into our cerebral cortex where they ferment — and, often, cement. We know most of our belief systems are deeply rooted and hard to trace. When new information challenges our belief systems, it does not mean the truth will set us free. Sometimes we need a compelling opportunity or threat to change our minds!

M. Scott Peck's advice to, "challenge everything"[49] may seem like overkill until we realize we're dealing with the currency of our life — our spiritual energy. Do we want to live our life with cognition and volition, or do we board some conveyor belt hoping this one-way ticket gets us where we want to go? In the movie *The Adjustment Bureau*, Matt Damon was encouraged to act with complacency to avoid pain and social stigma. Instead, he chose to act with conscious volition. The final message was a reminder to use our freewill or lose it.

In 2011, one of the first of several Internet-spawned revolutions began in Egypt — tweeting and texting. No one could have imagined such a reality before we witnessed this dramatic event. Fighting oppression and corruption, the revolutionaries were men, women and children who were willing to take a risk, to exercise freewill and co-create their lives. Even without the burden of political or economic oppression, challenging the status quo takes courage — until, perhaps, we realize *change* is the status quo.

Change Is the Status Quo

> *It is not the strongest of the species that survives, nor the most intelligent that survives. It is the one that is the most adaptable to change.*
>
> —Charles Darwin

In 1831 at the age of 25, Charles Darwin had a unique opportunity to voyage to South America aboard the research ship Beagle to study and catalogue specimens of animal life. The world did not know, nor did he, that his observations and copious notes and sketches would change the worldview on the development and progression of life on earth. The voyage lasted about five years. Darwin wrote, almost apologetically, that he knew what he saw was inconsistent with prevailing views, and as we now know, his work dramatically altered the way we understand the natural world.

After visiting the Galapagos Islands, Darwin noted, ". . . species change!" It was this revolutionary and controversial notion that led him to write *Origin of Species*. However, he withheld publication for nearly twenty years because he feared his views would be deemed heretical and would be buried by the church. In 1859, Darwin published his work amidst controversy and acclaim.[50] Today, more than 150 years later, *Origin of Species* is largely regarded as the foundational work on the development and evolution of life on earth — and, it is still controversial among the Creationists.

Throughout history, edge walkers like Copernicus, Galileo and Darwin have emerged, overcoming their own fears to challenge the status quo and seek new truths. These explorers accessed their own exquisite power to look at our world through fresh eyes, questioning and examining the environment in which we live and, in many cases, changing our viewpoints. Pilgrims from the scientific, theological, philosophical and metaphysical knowledge traditions are acutely aware of the juxtaposition between a changing world and changing perceptions. Ultimately, our perceptions create our experiences.

Change and Perception: Martha's Story

Martha is a fully qualified elder among us. Born October 14, 1918, she was 92 years old when we first interviewed her for our book. Tall, energetic and full of life, there is nothing feeble or aged about Martha; in fact, she drove to Kathleen's house to meet with us.

[To set the stage, when Martha was born, most people had outdoor toilets, wood-burning stoves and still read by kerosene lamps. Telephones and automobiles were not common for the average wage earner. Radios were available to families who could afford them. The changes in Martha's life are too numerous to mention, but you get the picture!]

We were mesmerized and enchanted with Martha's recounting of her life story — she speaks with clarity and sophistication. It would be easy to speculate this beautiful, gregarious and amiable woman had a comfortable life. However, Martha's countenance belies her modest beginnings.

You see Martha grew up in a small, dusty, rural Texas town. During the Great Depression her father lost his business, and forced to give up their home, they moved in with Martha's grandmother whom she describes as a powerful influence in her life. This move was one of Martha's earliest opportunities to experience both the casualties and opportunities of change.

Following high school, Martha met and married Walter Scott. Throughout their lifetime together, and continuing to this day, Martha does not live small. She joyfully recounted her years with Walter who worked as an agricultural extension agent, together traipsing across Texas during the Dust Bowl, getting soil samples, surveying land and raising their young family.

In 1943, during WWII, Walter was offered a position with the USDA in Washington, D.C. Without hesitation, Martha enthusiastically gathered her children and belongings and looked forward to this move. Four years later, they returned to East Texas for fourteen years. During this time, Martha continued to raise her brood and served on the local school board.

After settling into a comfortable lifestyle, Walter had an opportunity to move to Thailand in 1961. This was during a time of political unrest in that region, dangerous in fact. The Viet Cong were gaining strength in Vietnam and Cambodia was beginning to assert its power. Martha did not pause; she welcomed this new experience and refused to let fear influence her decisions.

For ten years she and her family lived in Thailand and Laos — reaching across cultural chasms, eating new foods and learning new ways of being in this world. Her children, educated in what must have seemed like very foreign lands, had the opportunity to see the world first hand — not through the prism of news accounts and history lessons. Martha's face beamed with delight as she retold stories of their experiences, difficulties and challenges. One of her stories involved getting food to U.S. forces behind enemy lines. We wondered if Martha and Walter worked for the CIA. Although gracious, her answer was guarded.

Martha never let her lack of an advanced education and humble beginnings inhibit or restrict her sense of living large. Eventually returning to Texas, Walter and Martha retired near Austin, where Martha remains a political activist. Her life represents both a thirst for and adaptation to change. When asked why she had never before shared such an interesting past, Martha replied, "because it is the past and I'm more interested in the future!"

————————————

In the last two centuries, we have experienced significant changes in our view of the world and our perception of truth. Take a moment to consider the breathtaking changes in science, technology, medicine and law over the past century. It seems ludicrous to think we can survive without changing; yet, we sometimes seem surprised when someone close to us changes. We often hear people comment, *s/he isn't the same person s/he was when we met*, or *we just outgrew one another*. Do we expect relationships to be anchored in constancy? Are we afraid? And, if we are, is it because we believe our spiritual essence and unique otherness is unlovable or are we afraid our partner's evolution will signal the end of the relationship?

Our lives are a process of change and renewal. Indeed, the order, balance and harmony of life are based on this rhythm. Spiritually, we evolve and change when we let go of self-limiting beliefs.

Imagine how our lives would be if we nurtured and encouraged the spiritual growth of our partners, family and friends. What if, instead of insisting on the safety of constancy, we became fearless advocates for exploring our own highest potential and encouraging our loved ones to do the same?

The Observer

> *The intuitive mind is a sacred gift and the rational mind is a faithful servant. We have created a society that honors the servant and has forgotten the gift.*
> —Albert Einstein

We are the observer. Right now, as you read this page, you are reading it with your rational mind but another aspect of you is observing you read this page. As an observer, we make the choice to either contain our experience with a rote, conditioned perspective or to let our observer roam through his/her intuitive, sacred space. Letting our observer roam is an act of volition — one we make when we allow our true self to manifest.

To act with volition requires we first consider our perspective — so we know what our choices are before we choose.

Take that old "think before we act" adage with a few new twists: let's consider our perspective before we think, before we choose, before we act. (If only there were a verb for the word volition. Do we *volite*?)

We rely on perspective to bring understanding, meaning and focus to multi-dimensional experiences. When we act with conscious volition, we are aware of the observer and better able to consider limitless possibilities. We commonly refer to this as thinking outside of the box. The box is not *how it has always been done*; it is more about *how we have always limited our perspective*. When we act with rote attention, or inattention, we are not aware of the observer, and rather than acting with conscious volition, we react with a repetitive, conditioned behavior. Thus, we limit our possibilities and stifle our potential for new experiences and growth.

Even when the observation is purely physical, we know our position or perspective affects what we see. For example, from the seat of an airplane, it seems as if the ground is moving. If we were on the ground, it is clear the airplane is moving. This simple example demonstrates how physical reality is affected by perspective. If we include the dimensions of knowledge and experience to this fact pattern, we know the airplane is moving.

Our perspective on relationships involves more complex psychological and philosophical constructs; however, it is our individual perspective that drives our behavior. Attaining broader perspectives requires we both trust the intuitive mind as a sacred gift and exercise our volition as rational, thinking beings when we examine our perspectives of self, others and our world.

Because our thoughts and perspectives drive our experiences, it's important we keep in mind that our perspectives are influenced by the beliefs, views, patterns and practices we've embraced over a lifetime. When we challenge these beliefs, patterns and practices we begin to understand how many of these *mis*perceptions affected our perspective of others and our experience.

To illustrate, if we view ourselves as unlovable, uninteresting, unattractive (fill in the blank), we often see others reflecting back what we believe to be true. Think about how this causes us to misjudge, misinterpret and under appreciate the people around us.

For example, if we are seated in a back corner, away from the windows and entrance of an otherwise empty restaurant, we might interpret this as affirmation of our poor self-image. Our *poor-self-image perception* drives our experience. In this situation, the hostess may seat early diners in the back to avoid disturbing them during the anticipated luncheon rush. In almost all cases, where we are seated is not about us, and certainly, not about our self-image!

As we continue to clean the attic and give up our old ways of being, we begin to view our exterior and interior journeys with fresh eyes — altering our perspectives and consciously co-creating our lives with both cognition and volition.

Freewill

The eye sees only what the mind is prepared to comprehend.

—Robertson Davies

Altering our perspective is a volitional act, an act of will. We have the capacity to consciously decide every moment of every day what perspective to hold in relation to our life and everyone in it. If we choose to see the world as good, people as good, we will find goodness. If we choose to see the world as dangerous, dark and unforgiving we will experience exactly that. As director and producer of our own experience, we have the freewill to act with volition and manifest love; or, let fear carry us away.

Because our perspective guides our moment-by-moment perceptions, it has a significant influence on the quality of our life. Perception interprets our experiences — the quick, acute, conditioned responses emanating from our perspective. If we plant Brussels sprouts in our garden, why would we expect to harvest radishes? If we want radishes, we have to plant radishes. When we act with volition and manifest love, we transform ourselves and actively co-create our experience.

Keeping it simple — when we consciously change our perspective, we alter our perception *and* intentionally co-create our experience. This is freewill.

Challenging Perspective

A wonderful quip from comedian Arsenio Hall is, "I have a life. I just don't use it!"

Although we have freewill to choose the context in which we see and experience everything in our life, most of us *just don't use it!* Let's look. If we see a dog in distress and our perspective is dogs are dangerous, the dog is a threat. If we see this same dog with a perspective that dogs are wo/man's best friends, the dog is an opportunity to provide aid and comfort. The same dog, the same circumstances — with two different perspectives. But wait, what if someone was bitten or attacked by a dog when they were children? What if they were? Does experience eliminate freewill? Or worse yet, do we want fear to control destiny?

Regardless of our experiences or fears, each of us has the ability to change our perspective. In this example, if fear keeps us from approaching the dog, our changed or changing perspective might lead us to seek help from someone who is less fearful. This new experience may be a way to *reframe* our perspective.

Discussion

Kathleen: *My sense is we have all experienced a change in perspective that was both immediate and surprising. Will you share one?*

Bonner: *I'm sure I've had many. The first that comes to mind is discovering my pastor did not have all the answers. It may seem like a small thing to someone who was not raised in the Bible Belt, but I assure you, the power of the pulpit was inviolable. Following a Sunday church service, I overheard my pastor disagreeing with something the visiting pastor said during the sermon. The visiting pastor asked, 'James, do you believe exactly what you believed ten years ago?' Surprising to me, my pastor's response was, 'Well no, I guess not.' The visiting pastor replied, 'Well then, would it be fair to say that what you believed ten years ago was wrong?' This event caused me to question the truth from the pulpit — a very surprising change in perspective for a fundamentalist Christian boy!*

Bonner: *Same question to you, any change in perspective that was both immediate and surprising?*

Kathleen: *One with real contrast! In junior high, my friends and I pirated a very tattered copy of the book Peyton Place and read all of the 'dirty' sections. For some reason, this caused me to become highly cynical and suspicious of adults, as it became 'clear to me' everyone was behaving in this manner and keeping it secret. I was outraged and of course, very curious about the human species.*

Kathleen: *I also assume many of us have had the experience of wanting to change someone else's perspective. Any memorable?*

Bonner: *Dinosaurs. My mother once confessed to me that the existence of dinosaurs always troubled her. Having been raised and taught to believe the earth was 6,000 years old, she could not reconcile her religious teaching with scientific evidence — the earth is 4.5 billion years old.*

Kathleen: *And?*

Bonner: *Knowing she was sensitive about the creation view, I said it was my belief the creation story was an allegory, but I did not challenge her belief about creation. It was one of those times when it seemed more important to listen than to ask her to look at evidence to change her perspective.*

Kathleen: *That's such a good point. We opened this book with the commitment not to proselytize and to honor everyone's unique journey. Yet, when we have information we believe important to someone else's perspective, it is easy to cross this line. What a good reminder to honor feelings and beliefs.*

Bonner: *How about you – any perspectives you tried to change?*

Kathleen: *Many. As you know, I am more apt to try to change someone's perspective. My most memorable is rather silly. My stepfather was convinced The University of Michigan was a Catholic school. I knew he was confusing it with The University of Detroit. No facts, publications or testimony by others changed his perspective. I went to my high school counselor because I was so frustrated by his unwillingness to consider the facts. Very wisely, she told me to smile and say, 'Really?' Still good advice!*

Kathleen: *What do you think gets in the way of broadening or changing our perspectives?*

Bonner: *When we cling to belief systems and become intractable, we limit ourselves. I know we like to think we are open, but openness is an illusion if we are not willing to consider new knowledge and shift our perspective. In addition, I think group norms and polite behavior get in our way when our interest is gaining the good will of friends, employers, congregants, and others.*

Kathleen: *Then, there's the broader aspect of what it takes to influence societal changes in perspective.*

Bonner: *Right. Within my lifetime we began to recognize the fallacy of both racial and gender perspectives that were once considered appropriate in the U.S.*

Culturally, we're finally beginning to appreciate how these discriminatory and oppressive views affected the lives of people who were not white, heterosexual males. Although we have made progress, there are still far too many who are oppressed because of race, gender or religious convictions — a source of conflict, chaos and pain. If we are to evolve, we must embrace our differences.

Bonner: *What's your experience?*

Kathleen: *You chose one close to my heart. Another exciting and important change in societal perspective is our developing global community. One of the most positive aspects of the Internet is how this 'shrinking world' brings us together in both our shared humanity and unique individuality.*

Whether we challenge our own perspectives, or society's, we have the clear volitional authority to choose how we will view our self, others and the world. Even those who are oppressed economically, politically or physically have this same opportunity to change perspective and experience life through their thoughts. Although freewill to act may be constrained, each of us is the ultimate keeper of our own perspectives.

Provoking the Pattern

Thoughts are reality and our perspective affects how we view someone or something.

Practice: Think about how you perceive someone — a friend, family member or co-worker. Then, consciously begin shifting your perspective by reframing any negative thoughts.

For example: If you think this person does not listen to you, reframe this thought by thinking: *This person cares about me — how I think and feel. When we talk, I will give him/her the opportunity to listen.* Continue this over several weeks and see if there is a difference.

As we co-create our experience, we find it is our perspective that leads — or feeds — the outcome. Sometimes, what we learn is surprising. In this example, we may discover we were the person not listening!

The Pilgrims

> *One who changes and does not journey is a chameleon*
> *One who journeys without changing is a vagabond*
> *One who journeys and changes is a pilgrim*
> —Mark Nepo

What distinguishes edge walkers like Copernicus, Galileo, Darwin, Einstein and others from 'ordinary' people? Is it superior intellect, education and opportunity or something we are all capable of, the ability to view life without *pre-conceptions*? As Nepo's quote suggests, these edge walkers were pilgrims who undertook the exploration of life as an adventure. During their earth journey, they were able to look beyond widely held perspectives and open themselves to the endless possibilities of the universe.

The simple act of acknowledging we live in a world of endless possibilities, where change, new insights and revelations are a natural occurrence, will have an immediate and lasting impact on our ability to become more awake and aware, navigate change and embrace our co-creative power.

The Fire Ceremony

My abiding interest and curiosity about Native American rituals led me to a practice called the 'fire ceremony.' When I moved to Utah, I immediately began to meet people who shared my interests and had developed their own practices for sweat lodges and other Native American rituals. It seemed natural to begin offering a Friday evening fire ceremony to celebrate this community of kindred spirits and preserve rituals that were indigenous in this isolated mountain setting.

The fire ceremony begins by blessing the materials to build the fire. Then, sitting around a fire, we begin the ritual prayers to invoke and invite the spirits of the seven directions and the ancient wisdom of the teachers and ancestors to join us in a meditation and celebration of connection to life and all living things.

An ancient spiritual DNA code has been built up over thousands of years of human history. The manifestation of energy from the creation Source still propels us into the future. Because the successful transformation of our individual lives, indeed that of humanity itself, cannot rely solely on what we learn — we must incorporate what we 'remember' as part of our oneness.

This process of remembering requires an integrated consciousness, a connection to the Source. In the fire of change, we learn we are not who we were before we arrived on this earth plane — and any illusion we are the product of a blue print, a grand architectural design or a printed circuit board goes up in flames! We are a vessel equipped for change. This is just as true when we are 62 as when we were two.

Our purpose here on earth is something shared by all other human beings — indeed shared by all of creation. Our purpose is to evolve. As Darwin describes, evolution is the process of continuous change from a lower to a higher, more complex and better state. I believe this applies to both our physical and spiritual evolution.

Sometimes change is forced upon us by circumstances and we must adapt. When it comes to perspective, we are innately prepared to change and evolve with intentionality.

—Bonner

Living in HD

As Carlos Castañeda discovered in his work with the sorcerer Don Juan Matus, one who lives by the Source has two primary tools: cognition, the ability to learn through awareness; and volition, the ability to act according to his or her will.[51]

When we act with intention, willfully consistent with the Source, and couple this with volition, we set the stage for co-creating our reality. Expressed in its highest form, full of its greatest potential, we begin to manifest our self in high definition.

Life energy is ours to direct and express. Perhaps more dramatic and evident when we see the results in physical healing, this powerful force affects *all* aspects of our lives.

At a recent conference we heard about a physician whose father had suffered a stroke and could not move the left side of his body. Each day the physician attached a broom to his father's left hand for twenty minutes and instructed him to think about sweeping the porch with that hand. After several weeks, his father was able to make small movements. After several months, he was able to sweep the porch with his left hand and ultimately gained use of the left side of his body. Super-natural? Do thoughts create reality?

Candice Pert, Ph.D. is certain of it. A well-known neuroscientist and pharmacologist, Dr. Pert is most noted for her discovery of the opium receptor in 1972 — the cellular binding site for endorphins in the brain. Yes, we produce our own opiates to relieve pain and induce pleasure, and according to Pert, *we are hard-wired for bliss!*[52]

In her mind-body work, Dr. Pert explains how emotions exist both as energy and matter in the vibrating receptors on *every* cell in the body:

> The fact that the word 'trauma' has been used to describe both physical and mental damage has been a key part of my theory of how the molecules of emotion integrate what we feel at every level of what I've called our bodymind. As a practical matter, people have a hard time discriminating between physical and mental pain. So often we are 'stuck' in an unpleasant emotional event — a trauma — from the past that is stored at every level of our nervous system and even on the cellular level — i.e., cells that are constantly becoming and renewing the nervous system. My laboratory research has suggested that all of the senses, sight, sound, smell, taste and touch are filtered, and memories stored, through the molecules of emotions, mostly the neuropeptides and their receptors, at every level of the bodymind.[53]

Think about the powerful influence of thoughts and emotions. How do you re-fire your neurons? What if we re-fired our neurons with conscious volition and intentionality? Why not?

CHAPTER SEVEN | THE COSMIC MUSE

Eternity is not the hereafter . . . this is it.
If you don't get it here, you won't get it anywhere.
—Joseph Campbell

We know relationships are important to our survival — to propagate our species and build and sustain communities for 'tribal welfare.' When we move to matters of personal growth and spiritual evolution, our relationships offer life-changing inspiration. And, we have many willing — and unwilling — muses on our path to enlightenment!

Moving beyond the Greek deities it once served, the word *muse* is both a noun and a verb. Here we refer to a *muse* as anyone who, intentionally or unintentionally, influences us to re-examine our thoughts, ideas, beliefs or actions. As a verb, of course, *to muse* means the act of reflecting or re-examining.

Who are our contemporary muses? Cranky, curmudgeon-like bosses, successful competitors, unrequited lovers or any of the many characters showing up in our lives — to help us see ourselves from another perspective. Like adding contrast to a laboratory specimen, what is and isn't there is hard to see without some opposite force, tension, emotion or opinion.

Friends, teachers, writers or poets with different outlooks often provide the contrast we need to move on. At times, desire or hunger nudges us into seeing the world from a different perspective; and on occasion, a catastrophe forces us to reevaluate what is and is not important in our life. Throughout our lives, a varietal cast of muses challenge us to examine our authenticity. Are we expressing our otherness, acting with conscious intention and manifesting love; or are we still relying on rote scripts, trying to skate by?

With each new insight or inspiration we sense the eternal rumblings of a higher truth calling on us to calibrate this new awareness, change our thinking and behavior. With each shift, each transformation, we integrate our own circuitry: the masculine and feminine, the pragmatic and spiritual, the temporal and eternal, our oneness and our otherness.

In *The Mystic Heart*[54] Teasdale discusses the search by Einstein and other physicists and cosmologists to support a 'unified field theory' to demonstrate the unity of the cosmos. Teasdale suggests the reason we are unable to prove this theory is because *consciousness* is the unifying force. Rather than looking within, scientists have focused on gravity, electromagnetism and strong and weak nuclear forces. Here, we consider the cosmic muse — *consciousness* — and how we participate, integrate and infect the order, balance and harmony of our lives and the universe.

The Spiritual Impulse

From our primordial impulse to survive and escape threats to our well being, we begin our evolution to higher levels of conscious understanding and curiosity about our earth journey. Andrew Cohen, an evolutionist, describes this state as our "spiritual impulse — the urge to become more conscious."[55] When we consider the merging of science and spirituality this urge becomes more compelling.

> *If there was any doubt at the turn of the twentieth century, by the turn of the twenty-first century, it was a foregone conclusion: when it comes to revealing the true nature of reality, common experience is deceptive. . . . What we've found has already required sweeping changes to our picture of the cosmos. Through physical insight and mathematical rigor, guided and confirmed by experimentation and observation, we've established that space, time, matter, and energy engage in a behavioral repertoire unlike anything any of us have ever directly witnessed.*[56]
>
> —Brian Greene

Unraveling the mystery of the cosmos through the lens of bio-suited beings seems so incongruous. Yet, here we are discovering new universes being born, stars dying. Amid this spectacular backdrop, we humans want to get a better bead on how we fit in. This whole idea of being part of the Source — being one with all living things, with the universe itself — must fit some rational, scientific or observable facts. Well, maybe not. Perhaps the mystery of it all is essential to our experience — to our evolutionary aspirations.

In *A New Earth*, Eckhart Tolle simplifies our experience by stating:

> One thing we do know: Life will give you whatever experience is most helpful for the evolution of your consciousness. How do you know this is the experience you need? Because this is the experience you are having at this moment.[57]

Is this about faith, acceptance or tempting the muses? Does conscious intention and volition influence or change our *experiences*, or does it only change our *perception of our experiences*? Is there a difference?

Are You Ready to Be More of Who You Are?

Early on, we asked the question, *What if our only job is to be more of who we are? Would we know how?* Since then, we've considered ways to unravel ourselves, discover our core and get out of our way.

When we change our perspective, we change the way we think and ultimately, change the way we feel. A life's work, our spiritual impulse to become more conscious, more of who we are continues to drive our longing for understanding — as we tempt the muses and continue our journey.

With the understanding that thoughts are reality and perceptions drive our experiences — it's time to reconsider ourselves as energetic, non-static beings with unfathomable potentiality!

Discussion

Bonner: *For you another muse is just around the corner.*

Kathleen: *That's right! Almost everyone I interact with has the gift and burden of serving as my muse. Rarely do I interact with someone without learning something about life or myself. Some of the most jarring revelations have been through telephonic encounters with unsuspecting muses in call centers throughout the world who push me to look at my crazed entitlement and ego-driven behavior.*

Bonner: *When we're challenged or frustrated, we often respond reactively rather than interactively or reflectively. How might interactive musing change our perspective?*

Kathleen: *So much of this interaction relies on us acting with conscious intention and volition. If I am awake and aware, I am more likely to listen and see others as potential muses. And, I am more likely to act as a compassionate muse for their benefit. If I act from love, I am able to interact and listen with understanding. If I act from a place of fear — impatience, entitlement — I will react to protect my fragile, misplaced ego.*

Bonner: *How does this work in our most loving relationships?*

Kathleen: *We (our egos) think we have more to lose when we interact with a loved one. As we know, the ego pushes for security and acceptance. When we have a temper tantrum and demand attention, this behavior is a sign of fear, not strength. Our ego is childish and looks to others to satisfy its needs. Coming from a place of love is mature. Great personal courage is required to stay loving in the face of conflict.*

Bonner: *If we see one another as co-muses, how might this insight affect relationships with family, friends and colleagues?*

Kathleen: *I'm much more likely to be a compassionate, interested observer — without taking someone else's comments as a reflection of my value or worth. Less reactionary, I find myself fascinated by some attribute or characteristic of the other person or our relationship that reveals itself for the first time. In this way, I'm able to give attention to what is — rather than what I make up!*

Bonner: *What about the less predictable, unsuspecting muses who break into our world and shake things up?*

Kathleen: *Encounters with unsuspecting muses are often more surprising and stunning. With less time to frame the relationship, the ego has less time to complicate the ongoing theater. Both the exchange and message have more juice and depth.*

Bonner: *You like to refer to shades of gray or ambiguity when describing your life experience. Why do you think it important to let go of the absolutes?*

Kathleen: *Because there are no absolutes. During my forties, I recall feeling wistful because some of my friends seemed to have such clarity about what they thought was good or bad, right or wrong. Life seemed so easy for them — simple. Later, I realized they were relying on belief systems that did not work for me because they failed to take in the complexity and richness of our diversity. When meta-systems calcify and become rule-bound, they tend to restrict rather than encourage the free flow of creative thought and expression. Naturally, my non-compliant self recoiled at the idea life could be guided by black-and-white reasoning — there were too many shades of gray to explore!*

Bonner: *Without seeing and navigating the differences — the ever-evolving, changing DNA double helices that guide our existence — it seems impossible to broaden our understanding and co-create our lives.*

Kathleen: *I agree. I can't imagine being rule-bound in this brilliant, mystical universe. I understand those who choose to operate with the absolutes of right or wrong, good or bad. Such a stance seems safer. But in reality it is more dangerous. When we operate from absolutes, we have a tendency to reject others who have different belief systems or ways of being in this world. We become brittle. The ebb and flow of ambiguity pushes us to greater openness and understanding of ourselves and others, and in my opinion, offers us a better chance for peace.*

Living with Ambiguity

We have all experienced some level of uncertainty, ambiguity and indecisiveness in our lives. For many, ambiguity seems to dominate the landscape, with decisions and choices fraught with doubt. Do we need these experiences to evolve? Perhaps. Yet, more likely our uncertainty is based on our tendency to think in absolutes like right versus wrong, good versus bad. And, because our earliest belief systems are based on absolutes, we grow up expecting life to operate along these bi-polar extremes. When we are faced with the ever-changing, ever-evolving nature of our lives and our perspectives, we sometimes feel lost and adrift — insecure. Both deaf and blind, Helen Keller is a perfect muse to instruct us about living with ambiguity. She offered:

Security is mostly a superstition. It does not exist in nature, nor do children of men as a whole experience it. Avoiding danger is no safer in the long run than outright exposure. Life is either a daring adventure, or nothing. To keep our faces toward change and behave like free spirits in the presence of fate is strength undefeatable.

As we mature, we begin to see the relativity and insecurity of our experiences. Provoked by our otherness, and growing awareness, we realize the polarities of right or wrong, good or bad, are relative and subjective — not absolute. Based on the perceptions of the viewer, everything we do and experience in life is *relative*, open to subjective opinion and judgment — our own and others. When we have the intent to become more aware of our options and choices, we find the power and energy to co-create our way through the elixir of ambiguity, freewill and choice.

The Masculine and Feminine

Are you male or female? Is spirit with or without gender? Take a moment to muse these questions and consider whether gender is important to spirit, to consciousness.

As you think about this, keep in mind that sex and gender are not synonyms. The historical meaning of gender is: "things we treat differently because of their inherent differences."[58] Although commonly misused to describe the biological sex of an individual, in 1955 the word "gender" originated as a psycho/social term referring to the attributes and characteristics society deemed representative of male or female behavior.[59]

This distinction between sex and gender raises the question of *inherent differences*. Are men and women inherently different? In his research, Carl Jung pursued this question when he attempted to distinguish differences in the psyches of men and women. Collapsing years of research and discovery into a few sentences, Jung concluded that both men and women held both masculine and feminine aspects. He identified what he called the "anima" as the personification of the feminine nature of man's unconscious and the "animus" as the masculine nature of woman's unconscious. Jung believed there was an emotional tension between the masculine and feminine polarities; noting these opposing natures come together in an individual's search for selfhood. Once the masculine and feminine natures are fully integrated, Jung suggests we reach a *paradoxical unity* or androgyny.[60]

In some Native American communities, tribesmen and tribeswomen who manifested both masculine and feminine aspects have been honored. Androgynous, they are called *two-spirits* (changed from the word "berdache" in the 1990s). Coupled with the belief that ". . . everything that exists is thought to come from the spirit world, . . . androgynous or transgender persons are seen as doubly blessed, having both the spirit of a man and the spirit of a woman." In these communities, two spirits "are seen as more spiritually gifted than the typical masculine male or feminine female."[61]

Today there is a rising interest in androgyny. Metro-sexual males have attracted the attention of women and the movie industry. Actors like Sean Penn and others who are more androgynous and comfortable with their feminine aspects are now representing the masculine persona. Yet, millions of men continue to hide their feminine nature, and boys still cringe when someone says they are acting like a girl. 'Man up' has become a common phrase used to convey to both men and women they are acting like women. There is still social pressure for men to act like men and women to act like women — based on religious doctrine or promoted by vanity industries and air-brushed caricatures of the ideal mate.

A number of thought leaders have concluded spirit is without gender. Eckhart Tolle states:

> In Being, male and female are one. Your form may continue to have certain needs, but Being has not. It is already complete and whole.[62]

We think our bio-suit is simply a vehicle for the spirit — with sex being one option (race, color, national origin, and even the potential for inherited creative talent, being others!). In 2011, there were three options for selecting the sex of an embryo: sperm separation for $400; sperm sorting by *Micro-Sort* for $3500; and pre-implantation genetic diagnosis following an in vitro fertilization for $19,000. The options for designing our progeny's bio-suits are not unlike the options for choosing a vehicle![63]

If we believe we are one consciousness, our body is a manifestation of this consciousness. Some refer to the body as a temple. Others, less reverent, might refer to their body as a Volkswagen! Whatever name we give it, our body requires our time and attention to keep it in good running order — but it is not who we are. Yet, we spend an inordinate amount of time, energy and money on gender, being womanly or manly. What does gender cost us in time, attention and dollars? In 2010, when almost one-half of Americans had less than $10,000 saved for retirement, millions were running off to see plastic surgeons. Headlines read: *$10 billion spent on cosmetic procedures despite recession*. The most popular surgical procedure was breast augmentation.[64]

If we consider the relativity of our masculine and feminine aspects, we find we are all on a continuum — some days expressing our more masculine aspects and other days expressing our more feminine aspects. Our vehicle may be male, female or transgender; however, aspects of feminine and masculine energy exist within each of us. What if gender was not such a defining issue? Would we give up the pretense of being someone we're not and spend more time under the hood?

Many scholars and psychologists have studied the question of gender under the auspices of *nature or nurture* and the debate continues. And, we wonder, does it matter? We tend to give a ridiculous amount of time and attention to the attribution of certain behaviors as masculine or feminine. What if we accepted androgyny as a more reasonable state of being? Instead of spending time and attention trying to determine what is and isn't masculine or feminine behavior, what if we each took this once-in-a-lifetime opportunity to be our self? Why not?

The Pragmatic and Spiritual

Ultimate Reality may be experienced not only through religious practices but also through nature, art, human relationships, and service to others.

—6th Guideline[65]

Sometimes it seems the presence of opposing forces in our lives push and pull us in different directions. This tension seems especially true when we attempt to balance the pragmatic with the spiritual. We find ourselves conflicted by the need to do certain things — demands that we see interfering with our spiritual pilgrimage. Then, in an effort to *bring order to our lives*, we tend to categorize our time and priorities in 'have to' and 'want to' buckets. Overwhelmed, we wonder how we will ever find the time and energy for contemplation, meditation, prayer or other practices we associate with our spiritual evolution.

The perceived conflict between our pragmatic demands and our spiritual or sacred longings are, in part, a result of the labels we use to define our activities. We seem to think these two kinds of experiences are mutually exclusive. Absolutes — one or the other. Joseph Campbell's quote at the beginning of this chapter reminds us eternity is NOW. If we accept this, we know our lives are not an orientation period to test-drive our bio-suits. We are living our spiritual experience whether we give conscious time and energy to it or not. Then, why the perceived conflict?

Carl Jung identified humankind's *duality*, or the seeming conflict between opposing forces, as natural. These opposing forces are perceived absolutes — labels of feminine versus masculine, pragmatic versus spiritual and other dualities we encounter in our quest to be more of who we are. In his research, Dr. Jung identified a process he refers to as the *transcendent function* where such dualities mature to represent a new form of consciousness, an integration of the dualities. We learn to hold the opposites!

The Lakota Sioux belief system describes it this way: everything we do, every action or thought is either 'ordinary' (*washte*) or 'sacred' (*wakan*). More important, everything we do, every action or thought can be either! In other words, cleaning the bathroom can be sacred and by contrast, praying can be ordinary.[66]

Thomas Moore frames this same concept when he talks about the soul as containing three entities — the Eternal Self, the Unfolding Self and the Practical Self — depicting each as separate, yet connected, and sharing common space.[67] Wayne Teasdale offered that unlike the *acosmic* (not of this world) experience of monks who devote their lives to prayer and isolation, our spiritual path is integral to our practical and peopled lives:

> Without doubt, there is great value in spiritual-ity that emphasizes and supports withdrawal from society. But in our time, with its special needs, we require a spirituality of intense involvement and radi-cal engagement with the world. It is in the real world that people live their busy lives . . . It is in the real world that their awakening and development need to occur, not off in remote solitude.[68]

Here, we have the opportunity to reconsider reality. If we quit looking for absolutes and stop compartmentalizing our lives, might we begin to recognize the natural integration of the pragmatic and spiritual? Would we then have the time and energy to manifest our spiritual nature in our everyday lives?

As we integrate the pragmatic with the spiritual, we begin the *transcendence* of our dual experiences. We realize the most mundane and common things are part of our sacred path. In Chapter Five we offered: . . . *job satisfaction has more to do with the love we manifest in our work, than the work itself. Whether you are a rock star or a stonemason, it is not who you are.* With this awareness, almost anything can be part of our spiritual practice. Consider the sacred-ness of planting a garden, cleaning the house, making din-ner, sharing a laugh with a co-worker. This is not complex — the idea is about bringing our authentic, loving self to our seemingly ordinary and pragmatic day. When we are awake and aware, we experience the spiritual essence in the simple movements, rhythms and obstacles in our everyday lives: tucking in a child, feeding the cats or sending a blessing to the rogue driver who just cut us off.

Think about the implications of choosing parenting, partnering or relating as a focused, spiritual practice. Is it possible these choices will lead to "the transformation of the human network, creating healthier, more balanced and harmonious alliances?"[69]

The Temporal and Eternal

In an effort to differentiate our earthly bodies from heavenly ties, a number of philosophers and spiritual leaders have attempted to draw a bright line between the temporal and eternal. Ken Wilber offers:

> While the timeless truths of Spirit are surely just that — namely timeless — it appears that the temporal truths of Spirit ceaselessly unfold, with new truths emerging daily, new revelations constantly accumulating, screaming surprises, jumping out at us from every corner of Spirit's astonishing creativity, as evolution itself searches secretly through the stream of time that is Spirit's great unfolding sport and play.[70]

As we move through our lives, it might appear "that the temporal truths of Spirit ceaselessly unfold." These temporal truths might be thrilling or terrifying until we question the difference between temporal and eternal. Is this another of those dualities we may want to integrate and transcend?

Many traditions hold that the spirit self is eternal and the physical body and all the accoutrements supporting our existence on earth are temporal. Are these temporal trappings part of "Spirit's great unfolding sport and play?" Does this unfolding support or distract us from our spiritual evolution?

Similar to the other polarities we've discussed, we think temporal and eternal are not at different ends of a spectrum, but more like a double helix carrying our spiritual DNA — expressing the divinity in all we think, say, do or create. For this aspect of our nature, it is like asking where we begin and end when there is no beginning and no ending. In Wilber's quote, he seems to be focusing on what we are discovering about the science of our universe and the seemingly endless inventive and startling discoveries. Are these temporal truths or are they the timeless truths of spirit revealing itself through science? Earlier, we said *all knowledge that is or ever will be exists within us all*. If we are one consciousness, how can we draw bright lines between spirituality and science — or between the temporal and eternal?

William Blake, a 19th century English poet wrote, "If the doors of perception were cleansed, everything would appear as it is — infinite!"

Our Oneness and Otherness

We revisit this polarity with new insight. Is it a polarity, or like the other imagined absolutes, do oneness and otherness ebb and flow throughout our lives along a double helix? Is it possible our oneness and otherness are perfectly integrated?

Among Native Americans, there is a belief that "All created beings are sacred and important, for everything has a 'wochangi,' or influence, which can be given to us through which we may gain a little more understanding if we are attentive."[71]

The Pagan God

Like urban legends, families have their oft-repeated stories —moments when someone said or did something that seemed momentously silly, crazy or unconscious. For years, I heard my mother tell anyone who would listen how I clamored down the attic steps to announce I had found my father's old Bible noting, 'it even has the New Testament!' I was, after all, a seven-year-old child who understood the word 'new' meant recent. Over the years, there were many more such stories to entertain family visitors and local shopkeepers.

Looking back, these stories reflect my earliest experience with my primary muse (mother) and my own musing about fairness, privacy, confidentiality and other concepts far beyond my childhood lexicon. My obvious misperceptions were corrected before I became an adult, and for the most part, these experiences taught me how to laugh at myself and move on.

But, it seems some misunderstandings survive generations!

While writing this book, I frequently talked with my daughter about our individual belief systems and how they have unfolded and changed over the years. One afternoon, she said, 'By the way — who is Beeth?' 'Beeth who?' I replied. She said, 'In the bedtime prayer you taught me and I taught my kids, we say, 'Father, Mother God loving me, guide me when I sleep, guide my little feet up to Beeth.' After calming my laughter and catching my breath, I said, 'Kirsten, the prayer is — guide my little feet up to thee — not Beeth!'

Two generations have been praying to Beeth, a well-intended pagan god. It tickles my giddy innards![72]

—Kathleen

Did the prayers of Kirsten and her children infect the universe with love, or did a cosmic mail daemon bounce the misaddressed prayers? Does it matter if we pray to God, Allah, Brahman or Beeth?

Curiously, religion is one area where our oneness seems most divided. James Hollis, a Jungian analyst, author and lecturer writes:

> It has been said that religion is for those afraid to go to Hell, and spirituality is for those who have been there. Any spiritual perspective that seeks to finesse difficult questions of good and evil, that seeks to scapegoat others, or that defers authority to external sources is an infantilizing spirituality. . . . Any spirituality that keeps people in bondage to fear, to tradition, to anything other than that which is validated by their personal experience is doing violence to the soul.[73]

Today, we watch conflict stream through the Internet, satellite radio, television and print media. Fear-based and ego-driven, we sometimes seem intent on insisting our world view is the *right* one. We reach for new rules, new absolutes to create order. Our response to perceived threats is force, our response to political differences is finger pointing or stonewalling, and our response to bullying is to reach for another rule. Doesn't this seem childish when we put it in writing?

In the United States, we sometimes take action based on a notion of superiority, often invoking God to justify the use of force to invade and occupy foreign lands. The media refers to it as 'American Exceptionalism.' As much as we want to believe we have discovered the *right way* of being in this world, it is not the only way. When we think and act in terms of absolutes, we create conflict. Even when we speak of *tolerance*, it is another way of expressing superiority. If I/we *tolerate* you, the inference is *you've got it all wrong*.

Whatever path we choose, religion we practice, or political party we endorse, we are one consciousness. The challenge is to appreciate the breathtaking beauty of our ever-evolving otherness. This is harder. There are times when we — Bonner and Kathleen — wonder what strange set of circumstances caused us to think we could write a book together. It's nuts! We are so different in so many ways; yet, as difficult as it is sometimes, we remind one another that our oneness and otherness may look like polar opposites but they are not. Each of us moves along the endless, timeless path of our double helix experience, trying to find our way in this world and express the boundless nature of our existence. Our otherness is just as critical to our evolution as our oneness. A duality seeking integration, we cannot experience our wholeness without our *oneness* and *otherness*.

Like each of the imagined polarities, oneness and otherness are perfectly suited for integration and we think, aMUSEment. Taking liberties with the word amusement seems particularly appropriate since *musing* takes us full circle. If we are both *one* and *other*, why do we continue to create conflict and chaos by trying to fit in or change one another? Think ego, theater and aMUSEment! Our oneness and otherness provides fertile soil for discovering our self in the cosmic order of our unique experience. Can you imagine a better plan for enlightenment?

Provoking the Pattern

When we think in terms of polarities and absolutes, we miss our chance to explore other ways of being in this world; moving from scarcity to abundance, fear to love, there are limitless opportunities to co-create our experience.

Practice:

Over the next thirty days:

1. Listen for absolutes in your own thinking or comments by others. When you hear polar opposites like good or bad, right or wrong, now or never, or words that convey extremes like never, always, all, none, challenge this thinking by looking for other conceivable options. Do not take action until you have time to consider the range of options and experience the elixir of ambiguity.

> For example: Someone tells you that if you want to make a career change, it is now or never. Is this statement based on fear — scarcity, aging? Navigate these waters to determine your own fears and concerns. Then, challenge the validity of these beliefs. Consider the multitude of options if you come from a place of love, your source of power. Now, reframe your perspective!

2. Reflect before reacting. Consider and honor different worldviews; then, decide how you want to acknowledge another person's view and if important, offer your own. Reflect on the belief system that seems to be prompting a positional reaction. Avoid acting from absolutes.

For Example: If someone challenges your liberal political position with a more conservative one, think about the cosmic muse, our one consciousness. Then, consider our individuated diversity. From a place of compassion thank him or her for challenging your thinking and acknowledge their position.

The Light Show

Unless you have a strong desire for melodrama, there is no reason to operate from bi-polar extremes. Polarities and absolutes are misconceptions. When we reframe our perspective to understand the relativity of our experiences and choices, we rekindle our light in a way that makes absolutes obsolete!

Now, imagine the cosmic muse laughing uproariously at something Buddha said — or was it something you said, or I said? Does it matter?

CHAPTER EIGHT |
WIRELESS CONNECTIONS

When members of the Blackfoot Tribe greet one another,
they do not say 'how are you?' they say 'how are the
connections?' or 'Tza Nee da Bee Wah'.[74]

Earthling moviegoers were seduced and charmed by the film
Avatar. Among the many mystical and fantastical images
was the sight of *Da'vi* humanoids and animals creating emotional bonds by connecting to one another through long tails
with wispy, filament-like ends. How perfect it would be if
we could simply plug into someone for the purpose of forming a deep and abiding connection.

Instead, we rely on our wireless capacity to identify, make
and develop connections with one another. Unlike promises,
commitments or contracts, the four aspects of connection
— intellectual, physical, emotional and spiritual — are the
bonding forces that sustain relationships. Yet, we continue
to believe relationships fail because someone is commitment
phobic or breaks a commitment.

Is it the promise, marriage license or employment contract
that binds us together or the connections we make and
deepen along the way? What if we shifted our intent away

from promises and focused instead on deepening one or more of our connections?

With great respect for the power of the Source, we begin to understand our power to energetically co-create and sustain intentional relationships through connections, reserving formal agreements and commitments to the more ministerial functions of institutionalizing these alliances.

The Mystical Nature of Connections

The Lakota Sioux call the journey on this physical plane *Wakan Takan* or the *Great Mystery*,[75] and from time to time, our encounter with others seems mystical, especially when there is an immediate, spontaneous recognition or connection, a sense that this person is important to our experience. In James Redfield's book, *The Celestine Prophecy*, he suggests such encounters are intended to help us find our way. Unfortunately, we often brush aside these occurrences, uncomfortable, not sure how to respond. Whether we pursue these connections or move along, the mystical nature of such meetings stays with us long after our paths diverge.

The San Miguel Experience

One summer, I spent a week in San Miguel de Allende, Mexico, with David, a poet I met during San Miguel's Poetry Week the previous January. Kindred spirits in exploration, we decided to make no plans and let the days and evenings lead us to new experiences and inspirations.

Our first outing was a luncheon with David's Spanish school classmates held next to a lovely organic garden at an equestrian center. As we were walking through the garden, waiting for lunch, a woman walked up to me and said, 'I think we are intended to meet.' Startled, I took a moment to look into her eyes. When I did, I knew she was right and replied, 'Yes, we are.' The energetic force of this connection was visceral. Before lunch was over, we discovered the many ways we connected spiritually and intellectually. Emotionally, our connection seemed ancient, intuitive. My friendship with Anna continued to deepen as we shared our most intimate thoughts, feelings and experiences — the loss of loved ones, our struggles with shame, isolation — and an exuberance, which sometimes set us apart from others. My connection with Anna was immediate and mutual; we were both willing to take the risk.

That same week, two others sparked similar kinds of immediate connections. One, an American woman who spent much of her life on the Gaza Strip, invited David and me to meet her for dinner where we shared stories about our lives, hopes and dreams. When we parted, she hugged me and said, 'You are my new best friend!' What was going on? Was it the effect of this colorful, artistic mountain town? The next day, we stopped for a late lunch. The only other diner was a young woman working on her laptop. I smiled and said hello. She smiled and introduced herself. Marisol told us she lived in Mexico City and came to San Miguel on weekends to write her book — on relationships! We immediately became co-inspirers and decided to meet for breakfast the next morning. There, we recognized our spiritual and intellectual connections. My attraction to her was primeval. For her, the spiritual path was to conquer the 'surrendering of our conditioning;' let go of belief systems that hold us in fear. This beautiful young spirit understood we are not looking for love but *nostalgic about it for ourselves. I did not want to leave, disrupt this mystical connection.*

When I returned to Austin, I told Bonner it felt as if I was living The Celestine Prophecy. Was it the magic of San Miguel or because I traveled with no preconceived notions about what or whom I would see, experience or discover? Do I miss these same opportunities for immediate connections where I live because I have preconceived notions about what I will see, experience or discover?

—Kathleen

Guided by order, balance and harmony, we find connections to one another are more about how we show up in our life — more about our openness to oneness than any external factors or forces. When we let go of expectations — what we expect to see and hear — and open our self to our own power and potentiality, connections will naturally occur. We then experience the bliss of our oneness and one another's otherness with grace, without judgment or demand for reciprocity.

A Satellite View

The desire for connection is universal. Many of us are in relationships where we feel connected by only one or two aspects of connection; others are constantly on the hunt to find like-minded partners, friends or employers. Sociologically, we are busy populating churches, political caucuses, clubs, consortiums, associations and social networks. Facebook is, perhaps, the perfect example of our longing to connect. See me, hear me, friend me.

Our desire for connection is also one of the most curious conundrums when we consider the concept of our one consciousness. In *The Mystic Heart*, Wayne Teasdale describes, "everything is part of an undivided wholeness where each being, or each conscious spirit, reflects the totality." Still, we often feel unbearably separate and alone. Unfriended? It's no wonder the epicenter for co-creating and sustaining intentional relationships weighs heavily on connecting, perhaps re-connecting or in Marisol's words, "the surrendering of our conditioning."

For many of us connections have always seemed physiological, mystical or magical; they either exist or not. In childhood, we were captivated by fairy tales of princes, princesses and knights on shining white horses. As adults, we sometimes continue this magical thinking, believing connections are more about pheromones, soul mates, star mates, past lives. How do we sort fact from fairy tale? What role do cognition and volition play in developing and nurturing connections?

Although there have been many scientific and psychological studies about attraction, which support the importance of physiological attraction for mating and romance; we were unable to find empirical studies about the four aspects of connection (intellectual, physical, emotional and spiritual). It's easy to appreciate the role of attraction in the formation of relationships, with its physiological and psychological firing of neurons; however, we soon realize attraction is not enough. Our longing for connection is whetted by attraction, but not satisfied.

There is no formula to form and sustain intentional relationships, no 'how to.' Like our own evolutionary path, each relationship is unique. How unique? Each must be at least as unique and complex as the sum of two different individuals. Then, as we co-create the third body, the "We," there is an exponential effect that heightens the uniqueness and complexity.

The beauty here is there is no formula. Becoming more of who we are — expressing our otherness — empowers us as agents of our own cultural and spiritual revolutions. We have the potential to form and nurture connections with the fullness of our oneness and one another's otherness.

On the Ground

In the film *Avatar*, the simplicity and authenticity of love, connection and relationship was captured with the greeting, "I see you;" a plain but powerful message to acknowledge the inimitability of one another. How important is it for us to see and honor one another's *otherness*? When was the last time someone looked at you and really saw you, knew you? If you've had this experience, you understand the transcendent power of connection. In a series of short stories about the fictional character Olive Kitteridge, the author Elizabeth Strout shares this experience, ". . . she had the sensation that she had been seen. And she had not even known she'd felt invisible."[76]

Harriet Lerner, a clinical psychologist and writer, described the integration of oneness and otherness by observing:

> Only through our connectedness to others can we really know and enhance the self. And only through working on the self can we begin to enhance our connectedness to others.[77]

We possess the wireless capacity to experience both unilateral and mutual connections. If I feel a connection to someone, is it necessary that s/he feel the same? Probably not, a sense of connection is a sense of connection; however, unilateral connections are typically experienced in passing, reminding us of our connection to all consciousness — to our oneness. True connection does not ask or demand attention. If we begin looking for, or demanding, reciprocity, the attraction is likely a fixation or attachment, not a connection. Here, we focus on creating conditions to develop and sustain *welcomed, mutual* connections.

Conditioning for Trust

Just trust yourself — then you will know how to live.
—Goethe

Common knowledge, contemporary research and current social lore tell us trust is *prima facie* in determining both the quality and depth of connections in our relationships. As a transitive verb, Webster defines trust, "to commit or place in one's care or keeping; to rely on the truthfulness or accuracy of, believe; to place confidence in, rely on."

In its simplest form, trust is a construct between two or more individuals who rely upon one another. From casual friendships (neighbors, local retailers) to highly formal commitments (priesthood, royalty), trust is viewed as an important foundation for continuing a relationship. As evidence of the importance of trust in relationships, our judicial systems, alternative resolution practices, relationship counselors, ministers, life coaches and other professionals have created entire industries to help individuals build or regain trust in the process, if not in another person.

In his book, *The Social Animal*, David Brooks suggests:

Trust is habitual reciprocity that becomes coated by emotion. It grows when two people begin volleys of communication and cooperation and slowly learn they can rely upon each other.[78]

Because trust is one of those heavily loaded words we casually fling about, it is important to challenge both its meaning and influence on our relationships. Is trust based on our own sense of self, security and wholeness or the actions of someone else? What if trust only requires we trust our self?

Certainly, trust is relative — not an absolute, not an end game. Trust is an evolutionary process and, like its human keeper, an easy target for the ego. If we haven't experienced mistrust, most of us have witnessed the chaotic effects of friends or partners who are unable to trust. No amount of good behavior, reassurance, attention or commitment seems to be enough. Even when we have the capacity to trust, it is often conditional.

Consider the following scenarios:

> Scenario One: I trust my sister with my life, but don't trust her to be on time. Because I trust her to make the important decisions, it seems less important she is habitually late. I make adjustments.

> Scenario Two: I trust my partner to provide for our family and me; I do not trust my partner to be faithful. If monogamy is important to me and I don't trust my partner to be faithful, it is unlikely anything s/he says or does will change my lack of trust. My perspective sets the tone.

Both scenarios are more about our ability to trust and less about someone else's performance or power of persuasion.

Over time and experience in a relationship, we may be more open to trusting, as described by David Brooks; however, it seems clear that our wholeness and sense of self makes trust far less provocative.

If we recognize our wholeness and have confidence in our unique otherness, we rely less on the actions of others and more on our ability to exercise volition and move through our lives with grace. Less inclined to drama, we are more prone to acceptance, forgiveness and choice — the choice to determine what is ultimately important to us in our relationships. When we are more secure in our wholeness, more trusting of ourselves, we are better prepared for the deeper dive in intimacy.

Getting Naked

To know someone deeply
is like hearing the moon through the ocean
or having a hawk lay bright leaves at your feet.
It seems impossible, even while it happens.

—Mark Nepo

The word *intimacy* dates back to the 1600s and was a euphemism for sexual intercourse. Today, in spite of complaints by women that some men are still in the 1600s, this word is more commonly used to describe emotional closeness. We see intimacy as a safe harbor to express our oneness and otherness — share our hopes, fears, dreams, achievements and failures. Intimacy does not mean unconditional support for all we say or do. Intimacy means we have created the space to authentically express our opinions, lovingly challenge one another and deepen our connections.

In his book, *Who Am I? The Sacred Quest*, Jean Klein tells us, "Relationships are the mirror in which your inner being gets reflected."[79] In relationships, we gain knowledge about our otherness — both self knowledge and knowledge of other; in *intimate* relationships, we gain knowledge of both our otherness and oneness. That is the distinction. Like trust, our capacity for intimacy is essential to deepening our connections. Not for the timid, intimacy requires maturity and the emotional courage to undress and remove the many layers of our fabricated, ego-driven self.

As we begin our discussion of the four aspects of connection, consider how the conditions for trust and intimacy begin from within. Taking the two together, our mantra might read:

> Because I am whole, I trust my venture into intimacy will not render me helpless. Rather, it will lead me to dimensions of my oneness and otherness I have not yet explored.

Intellectual Connections

One need only scan the social networks and dating services to understand the premium we put on finding someone with whom we have an intellectual connection. Advanced degreed individuals look for advanced degreed partners; high school graduates look for high school graduates. Scholars will likely want 'brainiacs,' others won't. For many, the intellectual connection is essential to successful partnering.

In practice, this connection is less about academic achievement and more about intellectual curiosity, energy and involvement. On the surface, the intellectual connection may seem the least critical and simplest of the four connections; however, it is the workhorse. It feeds and stimulates the partnership to challenge the status quo and explore new vistas — supporting communication, problem solving, decision-making and conflict resolution.

When two people connect intellectually, there is a sense of excitement and discovery. Conversations become playgrounds for creative thought and action. The energy is palpable. The subject of the conversation might be anything from the esoteric to the mundane, from designing a new home to replacing a hot water heater. Without an intellectual connection, the playground tends to be fallow and conversations parched.

Physical Connections

> . . . one cannot take pleasure without giving pleasure, and that every gesture, every caress, every touch, every glance, every last bit of the body has its secret, which brings happiness to the person who knows how to wake it.
>
> —Hermann Hesse, Siddhartha

More powerful than our sense of vulnerability, self-consciousness or, at times, feelings of shame, our desire to mate ensures the procreation of our species. Yet, we find layers upon layers of taboos, labels, guilt and repression when it comes to our physicality and sexuality. Some say our culture treats sexuality too superficially; others say we take it too seriously. Still controversial in the 21st century, discussions about our maligned and misunderstood sexual natures continue to cause otherwise mature adults to wince or blush.

In our longing to be accepted, fit in, we tend to compare ourselves to reported 'norms' and worry when we find we are outside the 'norm.' What if we stopped this limited thinking and began to consider how life would be if we looked at our physicality, sexuality and sensuality as a form of individual, personal expression? Might we then take delight in being different? Like other aspects of self, there is no one *right way* to be in this world – no one *right way* to express our otherness. In relationships, this is exponentially true!

Beyond the instinctive drive or desire to procreate, our physicality, sexuality and sensuality are very much a part of our exquisite otherness. From ritualized, uninhibited Tantric practices to monastic celibacy, many different cultures and personal preferences influence how we express our sensuality and choose or choose not to have sexual partners. In *Taking Our Places*, Norman Fischer notes, "One thing is certain; we must build our intimate relationships on fierce honesty about our own sexual needs and feelings."[80] And, as Jean Klein suggests these needs are based on more than biology:

> In a relationship based primarily on biology there is separateness. But the moment the biological function is an extension of living in oneness there is no feeling of separation. . . . In the expression of love, all is moral. You are a poet, an artist, a musician. You celebrate with your whole being.[81]

Culturally, our sense of freedom to express our sexuality and celebrate with our whole being is often shaped by social mores and religious dogma. During the height of the Feminist Movement, Gloria Steinem received much notoriety for her assertion, "I do not mate in captivity" — suggesting there are better options than marriage and/or exclusivity.

Fueled by the advent of birth control pills, this radical challenge to traditional thinking liberated generations of women to reconsider their own sensuality and sexuality, which had the effect of dramatically shifting societal expectations and changing behavior.

Regardless of such shifts, history is replete in the multitude of ways people express sensuality and sexuality — from the restrained Quaker's to the Mosuo people in southwest China who have few if any cultural restraints:

> Sexual relations are kept separate from family. At night, a Mosuo woman invites her lover to visit her babahuago (flower room); the assignation is called 'sese' (walking). If she'd prefer he not sleep over, he'll retire to an outer building. . . She can take another lover that night, or a different one the next, or sleep every single night with the same man for the rest of her life — there are no expectations or rules. As Cai Hua, a Chinese anthropologist, explains, these relationships, which are known as acia, are founded on each individual's autonomy, and last only as long as each person is in the other's company. Every goodbye is taken to be the end of the acia relationship, even if it resumes the following night.[82]

In 2012, a number of journalists reported that sexless marriages were *epidemic*, with one noting, "For many couples child-rearing has become not merely an aspect of marriage but its entire purpose and function. Spouses regard each other not as principally lovers and companions but as sharers of the great, unending burden of taking care of the children."[83] *The Kinsey Institute Report* in 2010 indicated 22% of married partners in the 50–59 year age group had not engaged in vaginal sex in the previous year and almost 22% of married partners ages 40–49 responded they engaged in vaginal sex a few times per year to monthly.

Although many tend to evaluate the strength of a relationship by the frequency of sexual activity, there is no norm. *The Kinsey Institute Report* reflects the many, varied activity levels and sexual preferences of our otherness.[84]

Another cultural influence affecting sexual behavior is the rising number of single households. In 2011, 31 million people in the U.S. lived alone, almost 50% between the ages of 35 and 64.[85] Add to this other shifting demographic trends, like longevity and the attendant physical limitations of an aging population, we see that celibacy may not be a choice, but a result of circumstances. Norman Fischer approaches this with creative aplomb:

> So rather than either being always on the prowl sexually or blocking out our sexuality because it has proven unsuccessful in our lives, why not affirm our temporary celibacy as an opportunity rather than a deprivation and use it to develop a greater warmth and connection to ourselves and the world?[86]

In spite of all this hype, sexual activity is only one aspect of physical expression and connection. When we express our *sexuality* we tend to act from a place of hunger, attraction and satisfaction: longing to connect and, perhaps as Klein suggests, attain the sensation of oneness. When we express our *sensuality* we tend to act from a place of contentment: seeking sensations of sight, sound, touch, smell and taste that distinguish our otherness. Both provide opportunities to deepen physical connections and express loving attention.

Regardless of our relationship status, sexual practices or proclivity, the vast majority of our time involves non-sexual activity. It is during these hours that we have the greatest opportunity to make and deepen physical connections with others.

The Oscar-winning silent film, *The Artist*, demonstrates how words and emotions are powerfully communicated through the body. Awake and aware, we are able to use our physicality to see, listen, touch and 'vocalize' in ways that demonstrate tenderness and understanding. It happens when we make eye contact with a tired shopkeeper, kneel down to hear a small child's story, hold someone's hand before surgery or share a hymnal with a lonely parishioner. We deepen our physical connections when we use our physical essence to offer comfort and love beyond the capacity of words, conveying our oneness.

Emotional Connections

> *God will break your heart again and again until it stays open.*
>
> —Hazrat Inayat Khan

So it seems. Still, we continue to risk the power and profundity of emotion to engage with others to form emotional connections. Some may consider this connection the most fluid and non-fixed, ebbing and flowing like the tides — one day turning our backs, the next day sharing a kiss.

Many of us grew up with the notion that emotions are instinctive or spontaneous rather than volitional. Is this true? If thoughts are reality, do such thoughts prompt our emotion? In his book *Your Sacred Self*, Wayne Dyer offers:

Your emotions are physiological reactions to your thoughts. These feelings show up in your body and they flow directly from the ways that you choose to use your mind. Your emotions do not just happen to you, they are choices that you make.[87]

Is it possible we can co-create our lives and relationships in a way that smoothes the sometimes treacherous white water of emotion? Let's reconsider reality.

Rewiring for Connections

The question of emotional trust has haunted me for most of my adult life, through two marriages and several relationships. Even after years of deep, soulful communications and close personal encounters while writing this book, Kathleen and I continued to scare one another when we emoted.

An old pattern, I grew up with an acute need to please — determined not to make a mistake, to offend or first set off my parents then later my partners. In the purest form of theatre, I became an actor in the role of husband or lover. I blamed my partner for any lack of closeness. It was her fault I felt disconnected. Rather than build connections, I worked hard to maintain the status quo; keeping the peace seemed the best I could do. As a result, I became a nonentity, unwilling to open my heart and expose my vulnerability. And, as Martin Buber offered, there cannot be a 'we' unless there is an 'I' or 'other,' to relate to. My disappearing into the woodwork was unattractive. Who makes connections with someone who isn't there?

It finally occurred to me that keeping the peace and avoiding conflict might not be a solid foundation for

*personal relationships. I began to look within and found
I was responsible for my lack of emotional courage,
emotional trust. I realized it was not my partner's job
to 'make me feel secure,' it was up to me to be whole
enough to take risks and establish trust. My emotional
connections grow stronger when I reveal my otherness.*

—Bonner

Eckhart Tolle offers a provocative view on the purpose of relationships and the importance of conscious volition:

If you continue to pursue the goal of salvation through relationship, you will be disillusioned again and again. But if you accept that the relationship is here to make you conscious instead of happy, then the relationship will offer you salvation and you will be aligning yourself with the higher consciousness that wants to be born into this world.[88]

When we act with conscious volition, we have the opportunity to smooth the white water of emotion. This does not mean we will stop scaring each another; it means we have options in how we view and respond to our own emotions and others.

In 1872, Charles Darwin published one of the earliest treatises on the study of emotion in *The Expression of the Emotions in Man and Animals*. Yet, after more than a century of study, the source or cause of emotion is still under considerable debate by psychological theorists. However, most theories recognize our ability to cognitively manage what we feel.[89] Whether emotions are spontaneous, instinctive or a practiced cognitive response to stimuli, emotions do not trump conscious choice. When and how we emote is affected by our beliefs, experiences, knowledge, perception and ultimately, our volition.

Yet, we operate in a society dependent on quick fixes: numbing our pain, quelling our fear, quieting our emotions with drugs, alcohol and, more commonly, prescribed medication. In 2011, the U.S. antidepressant market surpassed $11 billion per year in sales to meet the demand of a 400% increase in antidepressant use over a 10-year period. Estimates indicate that 11% of Americans over the age of 12 take an antidepressant, which includes 23% of women ages 40–59.[90] Although many have expressed a concern that doctors are overprescribing, mental health associations recently proposed that 'grief,' be defined as a mental disorder, to be treated with anti-depressants.[91]

Anxiety disorder is said to afflict 117 million people in the U.S. (approximately 50% of the population) with an annual cost of over $42.3 billion. Defined as "a reaction to perceived threats," anxiety disorder diagnoses rose 1200% between 1980 and 2011, making it the most common mental illness in the U.S. Although there are those whose anxiety disorder poses significant challenges to their daily life, about one-half of the diagnoses are due to "anxiety about public speaking."[92]

We wonder how medication affects our spiritual impulse to evolve, to respond with conscious volition and make emotional connections with others. How many of these millions of prescriptions are written in an effort to 'normalize' ourselves — to hide our discomfort —pretend we are someone else — deny our otherness?

Spiritual Connections

In our oneness, it might seem our spiritual connections just *are*. What possible act of volition makes or deepens this mystical connection?

> Out beyond ideas of wrong doing and right doing
> there is a field. I'll meet you there.
> When the soul lies down in that grass,
> the world is too full to talk about
> Ideas, language, even the phrase each other
> doesn't make any sense.
>
> —Rumi

When we make and deepen spiritual connections, we let go of *wrong doing and right doing* to support one another's spiritual journey. There is no proselytizing, criticizing or directing. Fear may arise when our friend or partner moves in different ways of understanding and being in this world, but we learn to counteract this fear with love — to inspire, and keep separate, one another's journey.

As a testament of our longing to make spiritual connections, we have built and consecrated churches, temples, schools, seminaries, communities, states and nations — based on religious or spiritual belief systems. Worldwide, reports estimate 5.8 billion people are affiliated with one of 20 religious organizations ranging from 625,000 members of the Rastafari Movement to over 2.1 billion members of the Christian faith. By population, the top three religions are Christianity, Islam and Hinduism.[93] The Pew Research Center reports that 44% of adults in the U.S. "have either switched religious affiliation, moved from being unaffiliated to being affiliated with a particular faith, or dropped any connection to a specific tradition altogether." The report further noted that 16.1% of adults in the U.S. are not affiliated with any religion, which is "double the number who say they were not affiliated with any particular religion as children."[94]

We are pilgrims — questioning early belief systems, exploring other practices, following our spiritual impulse to evolve. Joseph Campbell provides a compelling message about our diverse and separate journeys in his book *Thou Art That: Transforming Religious Metaphor*.[95]

> Apocalypse does not point to a fiery Armageddon but to the fact that our ignorance and complacency are coming to an end. . . The exclusivism of there being only one way in which we can be saved, the idea that there is a single religious group in sole possession of the truth — that the world as we know it must pass away. What is the kingdom? It lies in our realization of the ubiquity of the divine presence in our neighbors, in our enemies, in all of us.

Our spiritual connections seem the most vulnerable when we consider the continuing conflicts and wars in the name of religion. Why do our spiritual and religious differences — this aspect of our otherness — strike fear in the hearts of lovers and warriors? What if we began rekindling the light by realizing and acknowledging the divine presence in every person we meet? What if we begin by conquering our own fear of being left behind or abandoned?

Provoking the Pattern

There is an old story about the death of a Hassidic Jew, Rabbi Zusya. While waiting at the Judgment Seat of God, the Rabbi imagined God asking him why he was not more like Moses or Solomon or David. But, when God finally appeared God asked, "Why were you not more like Zusya?"

When we attempt to conform to the expectations of others, we distort ourselves. And, when we set expectations for ourselves, we often limit our experience!

Practice — over the next thirty days:

1. 'Show up' in your own town — as if you are experiencing it for the first time — with no expectations about whom you will see, what you will do or how you will feel. Expect adventure!

2. Practice 'seeing' others. When you meet a friend, colleague or sales clerk, look them in the eyes and see their otherness. With or without words, manifest kindness and attention, even in the face of indifference. By acknowledging others, you also acknowledge your otherness.

3. Act with emotional volition. Before expressing emotion, attempt to reframe your experience in a new way. For example, when you feel sad, is there something about the situation that is funny, tender, sweet? If you feel angry, you might decide to reframe the experience as an opportunity to practice forgiveness. Test your ability to find a perspective that will contribute to your sense of order, balance and harmony. Experience your own power!

It's Time to Be Strange

Artists, poets and writers often challenge the status quo and push for experimentation and authenticity. Now, it seems, our global community appears to be changing, albeit slowly, in its acceptance of differences and rejection of discrimination and bullying. Since we began this book, the word 'otherness' has become much more common, more relatable. Bound by our shared humanity, we sense an excitement about otherness. Are you ready to embrace your strangeness?

> *I used to think I was the strangest person in the world but then I thought there are so many people in the world there must be someone just like me who feels bizarre and flawed in the same way I do. I would imagine her, and imagine that she must be out there thinking of me too. Well, I hope that if you are out there and read this and know that, yes, it's true I'm here and I'm just as strange as you.*
>
> —Frida Kahlo, Mexican Artist (1907–1954)

CHAPTER NINE | **THE FIFTH CONNECTION**

We cannot live for ourselves alone. Our lives are connected by a thousand invisible threads, and along these sympathetic fibers, our actions run as causes and return as results.
—Herman Melville

In our quest for the 'perfect' mate, friend, employer, we spend an inordinate amount of time trying to fit in — meet someone else's expectations or more bewildering, attempt to change others. When we tire in our efforts to remake others or alter our exquisite otherness, we often rail against their ineptness or our own. Weary, we are forced to look within and take responsibility for our complicity in creating this ongoing mega-drama.

Then, as we gain an appreciation for our otherness and evolving sense of wholeness — we become less threatened by differences — our own and others. Once we make this turn in our evolution, we no longer want to change or clone ourselves but, rather, explore and celebrate the wonder and natural diversity of otherness.

Here, now, we read Melville's quote with new understanding and recognize the power and force of our actions. Ecstatic, we abandon the notion that connections are about sameness, shared interests or common ground and open ourselves to the richness of diversity and lightness of being: *The Fifth Connection — The Otherness Factor*.

Resonance Through Otherness

For most of our lives, we've been encouraged to *tolerate* differences. Title VII, the mother lode of civil rights in the U.S., makes it illegal to discriminate against individuals based on a number of protected differences. In response, businesses, churches, schools and government entities have developed policies and practices to demonstrate non-discrimination and invite tolerance. Affirmative Action Plans have been written and quotas met. These efforts seem very civil and respectful, but let's consider the implications.

When we *tolerate* someone's differences we convey a smugness that our way is the right way, which means another way is wrong. When we *tolerate* others, we distort reality, discourage connections and limit our potential to evolve. Setting up a competitive rather than collaborative environment, we miss opportunities to reach meaningful solutions in problem solving, decision-making and conflict resolution — we amplify dissonance.

Compare this to *accepting* one another's otherness, which conveys a level playing field where no one is right or wrong and all available information is considered in collaboratively reaching the most elegant solutions. Here, we amplify resonance.

The Fifth Connection, otherness, is a super connection that nurtures resonance to support our intellectual, emotional, physical and spiritual connections. Without this Fifth Connection, we get lost in mediocrity, fear and chaos. With it, we invite brilliance, love and peace.

A Cosmic Positioning System

The only real valuable thing is intuition.

—Albert Einstein

Instinct, that driving force essential to survival in the animal kingdom, is still part of our human experience — from an infant suckling a breast to our flight or fight responses when we detect danger. Interestingly, there is some debate whether instincts reflect a basic *drive for survival* or the *desire to continue the pleasure of living*. We much prefer the image of hawks escaping their predators to spend another day perfecting free-falling pinwheels and seamless glides!

Ecstatic Transcendence[96]

Summertime in Austin, Texas, is hot — a time to sit on the back porch and watch the world go by. A few years ago, two dark brown hawks entertained me with their free-falling pinwheels and seamless glides. One had two light tan feathers on its left wing. I thought of him as 'Two Feathers.'

Wherever I went, it seemed Two Feathers was nearby — at the neighborhood swimming pool, on short drives to the market or walks in the neighborhood. Although enchanted by the connection, I sometimes questioned my observations. Early one evening, I walked to the City Park and entered a Norman Rockwell scene — filled with baby strollers, dogs on leashes, children feeding geese and families sharing picnics under Live Oaks. The surface of the lake radiated sun diamonds. Off in the distance — a good 100 yards away — I saw a hawk. I stopped along the path and thought 'if this is you Two Feathers, come show me your underbelly.' Instantly, the

hawk flew directly to me — swooping up about five feet
from my outstretched hand. I saw the two tan feathers
and felt the enormous impact of our connection — our
ability to communicate.

Although I believe in my connection to all living things
— my mystical experiences usually occurred after dark,
alone or with a group of like-minded pilgrims. Never
had I experienced such a breathtaking connection in
a public place — in the bright light of day. This con-
nection was so extraordinary — beyond the limits — I
felt the ecstatic transcendence of my cosmic life force.
Uncertain of my ability to continue walking, I sat qui-
etly and listened to my strumming heart against the
flapping of wings.

—Kathleen

Once we get in touch with our otherness and act from our
authentic self, *intuition* becomes our driving force. We begin
to move through life like these hawks — unfettered — as if
guided by an unseen power. Life is filled with moments of
bliss — listening to a newborn's first breath, watching dol-
phins propel their massive bodies through water and sky —
truth and beauty!

Robert Bly captures this transcendent, intuitive experience
through poetry:[97]

> When the right thing happens,
> The whole body knows.
> The road covered with stones
> Turns to a soft river
> Moving among reeds.

Intuition, our *cosmic positioning system*, guides us to choices that create order, balance and harmony. Stunningly, ego-driven conflicts are quieted when we trust this sacred voice within — whether we call it intuition, the true self or rekindled light — it is our *otherness*.

Just Shy of Perfection

> *The imperfect is our paradise.*
> *Note that, in this bitterness, delight,*
> *Since the imperfect is so hot in us,*
> *Lies in flawed words and stubborn sounds.* [98]
> —Wallace Stevens

When we get out of our way, we let go of our fabricated, false self — the one we thought we needed to fit in or the self we thought would attract love into our lives. Once we undress and begin exposing our authentic otherness, we'll have some adjustments to make. Friends may interpret our calm, drama-free life as a lack of interest or a bout of depression! In the novel *Duane's Depressed*, Larry McMurtry's main character is a tough Texas rancher who, upon turning 62, walks away from his new pick-up truck, fancy house and melodramatic family. Settling in a small cabin, he walks everywhere in a Thoreau-like journey as he learns to live more deliberately. Almost everyone thinks Duane is crazy or depressed. Even he questions his sanity.

Duane's experience is an allegory for becoming more of who we are. As we consider the perfection in nature, our oneness with all living things, we soon discover the co-mingling of otherness and oneness is not static. Like the teaming, pulsating, evolving energy in all life, we change physically, intellectually, emotionally and spiritually. Each time we exercise freewill and act, we evolve. In relationships, each person promotes, provokes and remakes connections. At the moment we think we've arrived — attained some threshold of understanding — we get lost in a new perspective. A sense of being just shy of perfection is essential to our evolution. Given this, is piousness — the illusion of perfection — the last stranglehold of ego?

It would seem so. Why would we consider perfection to be static — something to be achieved? If we possess the power to co-create our lives — to think and reason, create masterpieces in art, music and literature, invent ways to heal the sick and improve the world around us — then being just shy of perfection, hungry for more knowledge, understanding, kindness, love, healing, is perfection! This message resonates in works of art that express the vulnerability and strength of the artist — where obvious brush strokes and imprecision convey the soul of the painter. In song, we find perfection in the seeming imperfection. The audience listens for the heart and warmth of the singer — the more precise technical voice sounds cold and aloof. In mature relationships, we do not look for perfect partners; we look for someone who is relatable, imperfect. Why then, do we often aspire to be the 'perfect someone' we are not?

In the *Immortal Diamond*, Fr. Richard Rohr suggests:

> Perhaps God and consciousness and Being are the same thing. This ever-flowing abundance that we call God clearly loves and revels in endless manifestation, fecundity, and diversity. The Formless One is forever seeking new and fantastic forms. Just watch the Nature Channel. . . . There is surely no indication of any divine interest in blandness, uniformity, exclusion, mindless repetition, or sameness.

When we manifest love, we express the ever-changing creative force of oneness and otherness. Even when we are at peace with the experience of oneness and otherness — we have not arrived. We are always arriving! From the book *Tenderness is Strength*, Gabriel Helig offers:

> We still tremble before the Self like children before the falling dark. Yet once we have dared to make our passage inside the heart, we will find that we have entered into a world in which depth leads on to light and there is no end to entrance.

Like other aspects of our self, the Fifth Connection, otherness, is not static, not absolute. Always evolving, otherness leads us to greater openness and expansiveness in our thinking and understanding — affecting everything we do, how we feel and how we experience life. Consider how your experience will change when you aspire to be *just shy of perfection* — longing for the next experience, a new perspective — the *liminal*[99] moment between sleep and awakening, another threshold.

In the Name of Love

> *Unconditional love is not so much about how we receive and endure each other, as it is about the deep vow to never, under any condition, stop bringing the flawed truth of who we are to each other.*
>
> —Mark Nepo

The course of history is littered with acts of treason, homicide and suicide in the name of love — toppling kingdoms, destroying careers and ending lives. The stories capture our imagination and entertain us — but these stories are not about love.

Love can't be parceled out as familial, romantic or agape — or any of the other labels we apply to feelings of connection. LOVE IS. Love is manifested through our individuated spirit, our authentic self. Kindness, attention, listening, caring, and supporting one another's spiritual journey may be an expression of a person's manifested love. But, these same actions may be the result of learned behaviors, instinct, neediness or other compulsions to please or gain acceptance. Does love elude us because it is more being than doing?

In his essay *Little Strangers*, Nathan Heller discusses Andrew Solomon's book, *Far From the Tree* and notes, "(t)he basic paradox of contemporary social thought is that in order to respect difference we elide it"[100] — meaning we suppress, ignore or pass over such otherness. In this context, Heller is referring to humankind's response to individuals who are born with physical or mental characteristics that depart from the 'norm.' Heller notes a growing trend to develop tribal unity among those who are considered different. Rather than accepting a majority's norm, minority groups are forming to celebrate and distinguish their shared otherness as a gift. These efforts are not so different from the Black Power Movement in the 1960s with the chant, *black is beautiful* — pushing society to an awareness and sensitivity to accept and embrace otherness as a new normal. Andrew Solomon's *beautiful ones* include the deaf, blind, dwarf, autistic, prodigies, transgendered — all different from their parents. Yet, within these tribes, differences *grok* differences. This growing awareness and momentum calls on us to let go of norms in favor of acceptance, kindness and love — to recognize how diversity unites us!

*Faith is opening, accepting and responding to Ultimate
Reality. Faith in this sense precedes every belief system.*

4th Guideline[101]

The Unitarian Minister and Catholic Priest

A few years ago, I had the incredible good fortune of sitting next to the Reverend Tom Rosiello on a shuttle bus from Leon, Mexico to San Miguel de Allende. Tom had been invited to give the sermon at the Unitarian Universalist Fellowship in San Miguel on 'Letting Your Life Speak.' We immediately realized we were kindred spirits and the one-and-one-half hour trip seemed timeless and effortless as we explored the mystery of discovering and living our true selves. Tom said when he recognized the incongruity between who he was and what he was doing he left his successful law practice to become a minister. His first career was built on 'the expectations and approval of others;' now, he wanted to support his true self (r)evolution! At the time, I was struggling with the idea of walking away from my work as an attorney, risking my identity, to write full time. Something loosened inside when Tom said he had been living his life 'from the outside in rather than the inside out,' trying to conform to some 'abstract norm.' We both understood the importance of supporting one another's efforts to become more of who we are. Like Melville's invisible threads and sympathetic fibers, it struck me that people show up in our lives when we are ready for a nudge!

The following year, on New Year's Eve, I was heading to San Miguel de Allende for Poetry Week. On the leg from Austin to Houston, I, again, had the incredible good fortune to be seated next to a man of the cloth. I introduced myself and learned I was sitting next to a Catholic priest from the East Coast. Older than he appeared, Antonio spent several years in Rome working with Bishops and Cardinals before making his way back to the U.S. When he asked about me, I told him I was working on a book about relationships. He wanted to know more about the book and I felt myself pulling back, hesitant to give him details he might find offensive. When I realized this was counter to all we have written about — I took the deep dive and began talking about otherness. After several minutes of animated discussion, he suggested that otherness with a capital O is God, otherness with a small o — the gift of our divine self.

When I shared my thoughts about love not being a commodity, Antonio immediately grasped this concept and told me he thought it profound, inspired. He said he would like to use it in one of his sermons. My sense is we both understood our exchange was intended — coming through us and not from us. The forty-minute flight was over in a flash and yet we had traveled so many miles to cross the divide of our respective otherness — small o — and experience our capital O — Oneness.

Connections, kindred spirits, shared journeys, are not diverted by religious cloaks, age, color, gender or any of the mien we think defines us. To the contrary, my otherness, Tom's otherness and Antonio's otherness bring us together in our perfect imperfections — as we journey on this earth plane. Who knew the Unitarians and Catholics had so much in common?

—Kathleen

In the name of love, we may choose friends and partners whom we connect with physically, intellectually, emotionally or spiritually. When we meet someone who recognizes and expresses his or her otherness, love is being manifested. When both have the capacity to express the Fifth Connection — otherness, there is less drama, less chaos and a sense of wellbeing — of being in love.

God, Allah, Ultimate Reality, Divine Intelligence, the Source — our spiritual otherness — IS love. When we express our otherness we manifest and reflect love — lighting the way for others to do the same.

Crossing Boundaries

Our spiritual journey is about crossing the great divide of otherness and making connections.[102]

—Jean Houston

Once we acknowledge and accept our true self, we are ready to cross the great divide of otherness and make connections. This interior journey calls on us to be open and expansive in our worldview. We no longer attempt to neutralize or marginalize one another's otherness. To the contrary, we recognize and celebrate otherness as a contribution to our collective consciousness — our oneness.

In 2012, at a U.S. Department of State sponsored delegation of mediators from all over the world, we heard from mediators in nations torn by war and organized crime or wracked by political and religious upheaval.[103] A young mediator from an African nation said he would welcome any advice the group could offer to help mediate the development of civil law in his country.[104] He said the Christians, Jews and Muslims each had their own set of rules, which made it impossible to peacefully mediate civil disputes. A silent still-ness — spanning centuries — filled the room as delegates contemplated the profound and ageless conflicts raised by religious differences. How does a developing nation cross these boundaries? How do we, in our own life, traverse the expanse of otherness?

During a London concert, Leonard Cohen recited the names of both prescribed and illicit drugs he had taken over the years — then remarked, "I've also studied deeply in the philosophies and religions, but cheerfulness kept breaking through . . . there ain't no cure for love." He's right — there ain't no cure for love. We are love. Yet, too many of us are addicted to the idea there is 'one right way' of being in this world. Driven by religion, politics, race, national origin, other beliefs or demographic markers, we take our beliefs, 'our one way,' far too seriously. When we deny otherness, we limit our potential power as humans and divine beings.

In celebrating our tribal beliefs, we often forget the power of love. Einstein proclaimed he could be an internation-alist and still care about his tribe. Caring and nurturing one's country, church, political party or associations is healthy. Insisting that one's government, church, political party or associations are the only ways of being in this world denies our oneness, otherness and evolutionary spirit.

Double Threads

> Oh God, that at all times You may find me as You desire me and where You would have me be, that You may lay hold on me fully, both by the Within and Without of myself, grant that I may never break the double thread of my life. [105]
>
> —Teilhard de Chardin

Teilhard de Chardin's double thread of life — his *Within* (Oneness) and *Without* (Otherness) — continues to seek integration. This is our uncharted, mystical journey. Our wholeness depends on this integration. Our connections to one another rely on this integration. How we co-create relationships and experience reality is driven by these two threads. Like the double helices of our DNA molecules, we articulate our life force along these two strands of oneness and otherness. Our common biology, spirituality *and* unique imprints represent millions of years of evolution!

The discovery of DNA has led to significant research in biology, medicine and social science. Yes — social science! "Your DNA is not a blueprint. Day by day, week by week, your genes are in conversation with your surroundings. Your neighbors, your family, your feelings of loneliness: They don't just get under your skin, they get into the control rooms of your cells."[106] Scientists estimate each of us carry 20,000–25,000 genes. These same genes reside in every cell of our body yet, at any given time, most are inactive.

Although scientists may disagree about the very definition of genes and the ways genes influence our lives — most biologists and social scientists recognize that genes, alone, do not make us who we are — gene expression does. And gene expression varies depending on the life we live. "*. . . We are architects of our own experience. Your subjective experience carries more power than your objective situation.*"[107] (Emphasis added.)

Challenging Reality

> *The mind is its own place, and in itself can make a heaven of hell, a hell of heaven.*
> —John Milton, Paradise Lost (1667)

The Genome Project to map DNA held enormous promise as a way to decode our genetic makeup. With this map, we looked forward to learning more about the human species and our individual selves — a crystal ball to both our past and future!

But, like the infinite, spiritual impulse to evolve — each new scientific discovery leads to a new perspective, leads to new perceptions and helps us rethink and challenge reality!

> Since the discovery of DNA in the 1950s, one of the primary goals of geneticists has been to understand how differences in the DNA sequence can influence human health and lead to diseases. After several decades of intense research, two conclusions are clear: (1) in most cases, it is difficult to establish a direct link between any specific gene(s) and specific biological processes or diseases; and (2) most traits and pathologies are associated with more than just one gene and have complex mechanisms.[108]

The *complex mechanisms* are epigenomes ". . . an ensemble of biochemical marks present on the DNA itself. These marks modulate the DNA's activity and functions, but occur without any change in the DNA sequence."[109] Gene expression is regulated by epigenomes which can be triggered biologically or chemically by environmental, social, psychological or mental stimulants — through memories, thoughts, experiences and heredity!

The study of epigenomes, or the science of epigenetics, has been around since the 18th century — almost 50 years before Charles Darwin published *On the Origin of Species*.[110] A "French naturalist, Jean-Baptiste Lamarck was the first to propose that surrounding conditions can modify characteristics acquired during a person's lifetime, and those characteristics can be passed on to the offspring."[111] Lamarck's work did not have DNA mapping to lift its credibility and was dismissed by the scientific community. Epigenetics regained the attention of geneticists in the mid-1990s and "only found traction in the wider scientific community in the last decade or so. . . . Indeed, in the space of less than two decades, the field of epigenetics has exploded."[112]

Today, epigenetics is shape shifting what we thought we knew about nature versus nurture — about healing — about co-creating our lives! "And, . . . your DNA itself might not be a static, predetermined programme, but instead can be modified by these biological markers."[113]

"Unlike the DNA sequence, epigenetic processes are dynamic and not fixed . . . they are strongly influenced by the environment and by exposure to external factors like diet, living conditions, exercise, stress, . . . Both positive and negative factors can modulate the epigenome."[114]

Our double threaded DNA helices are linked and re-linked by molecular motion as the steps in the DNA ladder continuously break apart and reform. This process of replication includes "cellular proofreading and error checking mechanisms to ensure near perfect fidelity for DNA replication."[115] Yet we are learning that our experience and evolution relies on how we re-fire, reinforce or challenge our reality!

Nature or Nurture?

Epigenetics is upending the controversy between nature and nurture. For years, behaviorists, psychologists and sociologists have debated this question. "Since epigenetics acts as a conduit through which environmental factors elicit lifelong biological changes, it provides a molecular basis to suggest that nurture has a strong impact on biological functions and behavior, in some cases, perhaps a stronger impact than nature (genes)."[116]

> All of these discoveries are shaking the modern biological and social certainties about genetics and identity. . . . *Gene as fate* has become conventional wisdom. Through the study of epigenetics, that notion at last may be proved outdated. Suddenly, for better or worse, we appear to have a measure of control over our genetic legacy. . . . Epigenetics introduces the concept of freewill into our idea of genetics.[117]

"Until recently, the idea that your environment might change your heredity without changing a gene sequence was scientific heresy."[118] Today, this idea is gaining scientific credibility!

Scientific 'heresy' continues to be challenged by the ever-evolving essence of knowledge, experience and growth. Epigenetics tells us that like other 'absolutes,' nature and nurture are not polar opposites, but merge and blend along a continuum to promote or provoke our genetic, biological, psychological, sociological selves. And, how we are nurtured influences the biology, behavior and experiences of our progeny!

Co-Creating Reality

> *We're constantly building and re-engineering new cells. And that regeneration is driven by the contingent nature of gene expression. This is what a cell is about. A cell is a machine for turning experience into biology.*[119]
>
> —Steve Cole

A cell is also a machine for turning experience into *reality*! When we practice visualization in sports, business, medicine, religion and relationships, we realize the mind/body/spirit's influence on gene expression. We have the power to nurture ourselves and co-create our experience by our thoughts — real or imagined!

Consider the times when we fake it until we make it. Whether we exaggerate our management experience in an application for a supervisory position, or push through fear to give an inspiring speech, we grit our teeth, visualize — create our new experience. Amazingly, we soon find we are no longer faking it — but performing at a level we once thought beyond our reach.

Faking it until we make it is just another way we use our mind and volition to co-create our lives. Every time we re-fire our neurons with images or visualizations of our highest potential, we influence gene expression and enjoy a new way of being in this world. If we do not consciously feed and nurture our gene expression, we give up our power to genetic imprints left by relatives — both living and ancient — perhaps dating back to our common ancestor, Lucy!

Although DNA is used to distinguish us from every other living thing — DNA is also the matter that joins us together. No beginning and no ending exist between these two entwined aspects. Consider this mysterious union of seeming opposites — oneness and otherness — an endless double strand — double helix — looping in and around us. Think about this miraculous energy responding to beliefs, perspectives, thoughts — offering both the world and its life forms infinite possibilities! The DNA ladder provides us a scientific and spiritual symbol of oneness and otherness; we can't evolve along one thread. And, like the universe, DNA precedes and follows its evolving nature. However, unlike the pristine, simple graphic — "real DNA, the molecule in your every cell, looks nothing like this. The real molecule is cluttered, complicated; you might miss the stepladder entirely."[120] DNA, with its expressive epigenomes, retains its mystery.

Humanity itself is bound by the double helix of life — past, present and future — its ever-evolving nature is timeless. Truth and beauty exist in our ongoing potential to co-create our lives, our relationships and our spiritual evolution. When Marcus Aurelius noted in the 2nd century that thoughts are reality, he had no way of knowing we would still be exploring this mystery at the biological, social and spiritual levels in the 21st century. Is it more astonishing that we confirmed Aurelius's intuition with biological evidence or that it took almost 2000 years to conduct these studies? The important outcome is we *rediscovered* subjective thoughts are more important to our sense of wellbeing than objective reality. When we feed our genetic expression, we guide our experience and co-create *our* heaven or hell.

Steven Cole offers, "Your experiences today will influence the molecular composition of your body for the next two to three months, or perhaps, for the rest of your life. Plan your day accordingly."[121]

Today's campfire for the *long conversation* is lighting up cyberspace and the global community. We know our thoughts are capable of lifting us to vistas far beyond our physical reach, deep within and without — as we co-create our lives and form intentional relationships. What is objective reality? Where does objective reality stop and subjective reality begin?

Certainly, reality is more than what we see! We form conscious thoughts about who we are and choose how we experience our bio-suited life — without ever forfeiting our option to remain open to our expansive, vibrant spiritual essence.

When we consider the whole of who we are — from every molecular motion in our body to every molecular motion in the cosmos — we know our life force is always moving, changing, evolving, replicating, becoming. And, as we change, flail, heal, evolve, the world continually rewrites itself.

Provoking the Pattern

Now I become myself.
It takes time, many years and places,
I have dissolved and shaken
Worn other people's faces . . .
                              —May Sarton

Consider the possibility of no end game — no heaven, no hell, no enlightenment — just more of the same. What if the power and force of our spirituality is about enlightening and not enlightenment? How will we experience our continual evolution, become more of who we are?

Continuing the Journey

In an earlier chapter, Albert Einstein referred to our sense of separateness as an *optical delusion*. The quote read:

A human being is a part of the whole called by us universe, a part limited in time and space. He experiences himself, his thoughts and feelings as separated from the rest, a kind of optical delusion of his consciousness.

Now, consider the rest of Einstein's realization:

> This delusion is a kind of prison for us, restricting us to our personal desires and to affection for a few persons nearest to us. Our task must be to free ourselves from this prison by *widening our circle of compassion* to embrace all living creatures and the whole of nature in its beauty. (Emphasis added.)

Twenty years after the formation of the *Snowmass Interreligious Conference*, Fr. Thomas Keating widened the circle of compassion and convened what is now called the *Snowmass Inter-Spiritual Dialogue*. This change was made to invite greater diversity, inclusion and broader focus. Going from *Interreligious* to *Inter-Spiritual* signals a tectonic shift in honoring otherness and liberalizing the exchange of thoughts, perspectives and perceptions.

The Fifth Connection, *The Otherness Factor*, liberates us to express our authentic selves and removes the ongoing conflict of expecting something different or someone else. With this knowledge and awareness, we are free to endlessly widen *our circle of compassion*. Richard Rohr captures our capacity for compassion by noting:

> Love, which is nothing more than endless life, is luring us forward, because 'love is what we also and already are' and we are drawn to the fullness of our own being.[122]

Love, our *endless life*, keeps us in a state of wonder — igniting our desire to seek truth and beauty — to experience order, balance and harmony. Each of us has an open invitation to manifest otherness, deepen connections and co-create intentional relationships that infect the universe with love. There is no expiration date, no *one right way*, no norm.

In Joseph Campbell's words, "The privilege of a lifetime is being who you are."

end

ACKNOWLEDGMENTS

The Otherness Factor could not have been written without the accretion of our collective experiences with willing and unwilling muses over our lifetimes and the many thought leaders whose work inspired our journey.

Special thanks to our *Unpaid but Illustrious Editorial Staff*—Sandra Whitener, Kirsten McLean and Jason Knight who hung in there through multiple drafts for more than five years and to Brian Pyle who joined us between his deployments to Iraq and Afghanistan.

In addition, we want to thank readers and muses in Austin, Texas, who provided invaluable feedback: *The Vino Libra Book Club*; *The Burning Bread Focus Group*; *The Inkslingers Writing Group*; and the *South Austin Spiritual Book Club*.

Grateful appreciation to friends, colleagues and muses, including Martha Scott, Kass Atkinson, Sharon Dent, Laura Pyle, Peggy Kelsey, Susan Bradshaw, Kathy Shingleton, Georgia Thomas, Ursula & Joel Brand, Charlie & Frank Cooley, Jan Penley, Jenny Blue, Pamela Hutchins, Leona Renfoe, Vickie Reeves, Danielle Brown and many others who provided insight, editorial comment, encouragement and nourishment!

We had the remarkable fortune of teaming up with Debra Winegarten, copy/content editing; Danielle Hartman Acee, line editing and social media development; and Kenneth Benson for interior design consulting and printing/technology support. The baptismal dressing, our book cover was designed by Mayapriya Long, whose creative translation *is* a hymn.

Finally, a special shout out and gratitude to Loren Stell and Tony Zito whose final cover-to-cover reads, editorial advice and pre-publication reviews prepared us for this launch.

The connections we formed along the way had everything to do with the brilliance of otherness and the power of kindness.

Throughout our work on this manuscript, we were blessed with the intelligence, talent, creativity and love of *others*, who morphed into a motley crew of good-natured, boisterous sideline coaches — cheering us on, lighting fires and encouraging us to *finish the book*!

Is it ever finished?

ENDNOTES

PROLOGUE

1. The word *Source* is used to convey our spiritual connection regardless of religious or spiritual beliefs. The *Source* may refer to God, Oneness, Higher Consciousness, Divine Intelligence, Intent, Field of Intention, Atman, Buddha, Ultimate Reality, soul, spirit; any term used to express the spiritual essence of one's true nature.

CHAPTER ONE

2. Peck, M. Scott, *The Road Less Traveled*, New York, NY, Touchstone, 1978, p. 194.

3. See, www.snowmass.org, web site for St. Benedict's Monastery, 1012 Monastery Road, Snowmass, Colorado, February 7, 2013. This cite reports Fr. Keating *continues to write and lecture on the contemplative life and to support the worldwide work of Contemplative Outreach.*

4. *Guidelines for Interreligious Understanding: Points of Agreement or Similarity*, in Joel Verluis, ed., *A Sourcebook for Earth's Community of Religions* (Grand Rapids, MI; CoNexus Press, 1995), 148; and Thomas Keating, *Speaking of Silence*, 126–29, which contains only the guidelines. For simplicity's sake, the

later edition found in the *Sourcebook* will be followed. It is a refinement, and in some respects, a rewording of the original guidelines.

5. Tiller, William, PhD., a quantum physicist who appeared in the 2004 film *What the Bleep Do We Know?* is a professor emeritus of Materials Science and Engineering at Stanford University. Dr. Tiller has published a number of books including: *Conscious Acts of Creation, Science and Human Transformation, Psychoenergetic Science*. Dr. Tiller was a recipient of the Guggenheim Fellowship grant for Natural sciences – Engineering. He is a Physics Fellow of the American Association for the Advancement of Science.

6. Dyer, Wayne W., *The Power of Intention: learning to co-create your world your way*. Carlsbad, California, Hay House, Inc., 2004.

7. Teasdale, Wayne, *The Mystic Heart*, Novato, California, New World Library, 1999, p. 76.

8. Tiller, William, PhD., a quantum physicist who appeared in the 2004 film, *What the Bleep Do We Know?* is a professor emeritus of Materials Science and Engineering at Stanford University. Dr. Tiller has published a number of books including: *Conscious Acts of Creation, Science and Human Transformation, Psychoenergetic Science*. Dr. Tiller was a recipient of the Guggenheim Fellowship grant for Natural Sciences – Engineering. He is a Physics Fellow of the American Association for the Advancement of Science.

CHAPTER TWO

9. See, www.just.NASA.gov as of March 20, 2013.

10. Eckhart Tolle is the author of several books, including: *A New Earth, Awakening to Your Life's Purpose: The Power of Now*,

Practicing the Power of Now and Stillness Speaks. In his works he discusses his spontaneous awakening.

11. *Guidelines for Interreligious Understanding: Points of Agreement or Similarity*, in Joel Verluis, ed., *A Sourcebook for Earth's Community of Religions* (Grand Rapids, MI; CoNexus Press, 1995), 148; and Thomas Keating, *Speaking of Silence*, 126–29, which contains only the guidelines. For simplicity's sake, the later edition found in the *Sourcebook* will be followed. It is a refinement, and in some respects a rewording of the original guidelines.

CHAPTER THREE

12. Rinpoche, Sogyal, *The Tibetan Book of Living and Dying*, HarperCollins, 2002, p. 120.

13. Dyer, Wayne. *Your Sacred Self*, Hay House, 2004.

14. Baruch, Bnei, www. sciences360.com/index.php/carl-g-jung-archetypes-of-the-collective-unconscious, March 20, 2007.

15. Cliff Notes are summaries of required reading in schools and universities. Students sometimes rely on Cliff Notes or supplement their reading with Cliff Notes to write a paper or sit for an exam.

16. Castaneda, Carlos, *The Active Side of Infinity*, HarperCollins, January 2000.

17. *Guidelines for Interreligious Understanding: Points of Agreement or Similarity*, in Joel Verluis, ed., *A Sourcebook for Earth's Community of Religions*; Grand Rapids, MI; CoNexus Press, 1995, p. 148.

18. DeFoore, W. G., www.goodfinding.com, June 2013, Vol. 7, No. 6.

19. Nepo, Mark, *The Exquisite Risk*, Crown Publishing Group, December 2007, p. 31.

20. Guidelines for Interreligious Understanding: Points of Agreement or Similarity, in Joel Verluis, ed., A Sourcebook for Earth's Community of Religions; Grand Rapids, MI; CoNexus Press, 1995, p. 148.

21. Coelho, Paulo, *The Witch of Portobello*, HarperCollins, February 2008, p. 150.

22. Teasdale, Wayne, *The Mystic Heart*, The New World Library, October 2010.

23. National Science Foundation, at www.neuroskeptic.blogspot.com, February 13, 2013.

CHAPTER FOUR

24. *The Secret Life of Walter Mitty* is a short story by James Thurber. The most famous of Thurber's stories, it first appeared in *The New Yorker* on March 18, 1939. *The Secret Life of Walter Mitty* was made into a movie in 1947, then again in 2013. See www.newyorker.com/magazine/1939/03/18. See also, www.thurberhouse.org/james-thurber.html.

25. Hochswender, Woody; Martin, Greg; Morino, Ted; *The Buddha in Your Mirror*, Middleway Press, October 2001.

26. Nepo, Mark, *The Exquisite Risk*, Crown Publishing Group, December 2007, p. 153.

27. Forest Institute of Professional Psychology; cite attributed to Jennifer Baker at www.divorcerate.org.

CHAPTER FIVE

28. Williamson, Marianne, *A Return to Love: Reflections on the Principles of a Course in Miracles*, HarperCollins, 1992, Chapter 7, Section 3.

29. Thank you Stephen Colbert for coining this word! In *thoughtyness* we are easily mistaken.

30. Hawkins, David R. *Power vs. Force: The Hidden Determinants of Human Behavior*, Carlsbad, California, Hay House Inc., 2002, p. 220.

31. Teasdale, Wayne, *A Monk in the World*, Novato, California, New World Library, 2002, p. 106.

32. *Identity* might be tied to either wealth or poverty. In poverty, some believe they are defined by their lack of money, property or possessions.

33. *A Progeny Story* is a story by one of our offspring. Between us, we have 10 children/step-children and eighteen grandchildren. We did not think it essential to introduce them individually; however, their lives with an Edge Walker as a parent or grandparent have led to stories we think readers may find interesting in our collective journey.

34. Hawkins, David R., *Power vs. Force: The Hidden Determinants of Human Behavior*, Carlsbad, California, Hay House Inc., 2002, p. 12.

35. Defined as: *the study of muscles and their movements, esp. as applied to physical conditioning* [Gk. Kinesis, movement (kinein, to move + -logy];" American Heritage Dictionary, Houghton Mifflin, 1987.

36. Hawkins, David R., *Power vs. Force: The Hidden Determinants of Human Behavior*, Carlsbad, California, Hay House Inc., 2002, p. 128.

37. *Guidelines for Interreligious Understanding: Points of Agreement or Similarity*, in Joel Verluis, ed., *A Sourcebook for Earth's Community of Religions* (Grand Rapids, MI; CoNexus Press, 1995), 148; and Thomas Keating, *Speaking of Silence*, 126–29, which contains only the guidelines. For simplicity's sake, the later edition found in the *Sourcebook* will be followed. It is a refinement, and in some respects a rewording of the original guidelines.

38. Hall, Kathleen, words from her poem *Begin Again*.

39. Teasdale, Wayne, *The Mystic Heart*, Novato, California, New World Library, 1999, p. 216.

40. Teasdale, Wayne, *The Mystic Heart*, Novato, California, New World Library, 1999, p. 123.

41. Acceptance and forgiveness do not, in any way, imply staying in an abusive relationship. We encourage any person in an abusive relationship to seek help and find a safe place to pursue life.

42. Audlin, James David, *Circle of Life*, Clear Light Publishing, October 2005, p. 83.

43. Tolle, Eckhart, *The Power of Now*. Novato, California, New World Library, 1999, pp. 154–155.

CHAPTER SIX

44. The Galileo Project, www.galileo.rice.edu, last update 1995.

45. See, http://www.huffingtonpost.com/2008/12/23/vatican-rewrites-history_n_153232.html

46. The Galileo Project, www.galileo.rice.edu, last update 1995.

47. CBS News, *The King's Popularity Constant*. See www.cbsnews.com/new/the-kings-popularity-constant, CBS Interactive Inc., as of March 5, 2013.

48. See, www.goseewrite.com/2011/02/traveling-and-dying-the-real-risks-in-life/#

49. Peck, M. Scott, *The Road Less Traveled*, New York, NY. Touchstone, 1978.

50. Helligman, Deborah, *Charles and Emma: The Darwins' Leap of Faith*, Henry Holt and Company, LLC, New York, NY, 2009.

51. Castaneda, Carlos, *The Active Side of Infinity*, HarperCollins, January 2000.

52. Candace Pert, a neuroscientist, was best known for her work in discovering the opiate receptor in 1978. She is also well known for her appearance in the movie *What the Bleep Do We Know?* The author of *Molecules of Emotion: The Science Behind Mind-Body Medicine*, Dr. Pert was a major proponent of alternative medicine and the body's ability to heal itself. Dr. Pert died September 12, 2014.

53. Pert, Candace, *Molecules of Emotion: The Science Between Mind-Body Medicine*. Scribner, 1999.

CHAPTER SEVEN

54. Teasdale, Wayne, The Mystic Heart, Novato, California, New World Library, 1999, pp. 72–73.

55. Cohen, Andrew, EnlightenNext: The Magazine for Evolutionaries, Issue 47, 2011.

56. Greene, Brian PhD, The Hidden Reality, 'The Preface,' Knopf Doubleday, January 2011.

57. Tolle, Eckhart, A New Earth, Penguin Group (USA), January 2008, p. 41.

58. In the Teutonic word, as in Latin genus and Greek γένος three main senses appear, (1) race or stock, (2) class or kind, (3) gender or sex, The Oxford Dictionary.

59. Sexologist John Money introduced the distinction between biological sex and gender as a role in 1955. See, Encyclopedia Britannica at www.britannica/EBchecked/topic/1240912/ john-money-John Money (American Psychologist).

60. Baruch, Bnei, www.sciences360.com/index.php/carl-g-jung-archetypes-of-the-collective-unconscious, March 20, 2007.

61. Williams, Walter L. at www.the guardian.com/music/2010/ Oct/11/two-spirit-people-north-america.

62. Tolle, Eckhart, The Power of Now, Novato, California, New World Library, 1999, p. 173.

63. See, www.genderselection101.com/gender-selection-cost. htm.

64. CNN Politics Blog, Cafferty File. Internet March 10, 2010.

65. Guidelines for Interreligious Understanding: Points of Agreement or Similarity, in Joel Verluis, ed., A Sourcebook for Earth's Community of Religions; Grand Rapids, MI; CoNexus Press, 1995, p. 148.

66. Audlin, James David, The Circle of Life, Clear Light Publishing, October 2005.

67. Moore, Thomas, Dark Night of the Soul, Doubleday Religious, March 2005, p. 35.

68. Teasdale, Wayne, Living as a Monk in the World, New World Library, August 2002, Introduction, p. xxiii.

69. The Otherness Factor, Prologue.

70. Teasdale, Wayne, Living as a Monk in the World; Foreword by Ken Wilber, New World Library, Spring 2002, p. xviii.

71. Nepo, Mark, The Exquisite Risk, Crown Publishing Group, December 2007, p. 107.

72. The phrase 'tickles the giddy innards' has been attributed to Lee Glickstein, a speaking coach from San Francisco.

73. Hollis, James, Finding Meaning in the Second Half of Life: How to Finally, Really Grow Up, New York, NY, Gotham Books, 2005, p. 186.

74. Nepo, Mark, *The Exquisite Risk*, Crown Publishing Group, December 2007, p. 107.

75. See, www.thewildwest.org/nativeamericans/nativeamerican religion/100-lakotaindiansconceptofwakan.html

76. Strout, Elizabeth, *Olive Kitteridge*, Random House Trade Paperback Edition, 2008, p. 213.

77. See, www.goodreads.com/quotes/136386. November 6, 2012.

78. Brooks, David, *The Social Animal*, Random House, March 2011, p. 155.

79. Klein, Jean, *Who am I? The Sacred Quest*, Non-Duality Press, July 2006, p. 21.

80. Fischer, Norman, *Taking Our Places: The Buddhist Path to Truly Growing Up*, New York, NY, HarperCollins, 2004, p. 161.

81. Klein, Jean, *Who am I? The Sacred Quest*, Non-Duality Press, July 2006, p. 27.

82. Bolick, Kate, *All the Single Ladies*, The Atlantic, Web version, November 2011, p. 4.

83. Flanagan, Caitlin, *The Wifely Duty*, *The Atlantic Monthly*, January/February 2003, Vol. 291, No. 171–181.

84. The Kinsey Institute Web site, *Frequently Asked Sexuality Questions to The Kinsey Institute*, last updated July 21, 2012.

85. Klinenberg, Eric, *GOING SOLO, The Extraordinary Rise and Surprising Appeal of Living Alone*, New York, NY, The Penguin Press, 2012, Introduction.

86. Fischer, Norman, *Taking Our Places: The Buddhist Path to Truly Growing Up*, New York, NY, HarperCollins, 2004, p. 163.

87. Dyer, Wayne, *Your Sacred Self*, New York, NY, Harper Paperbacks, 1995, p. 328.

88. Tolle, Eckhart, *The Power of Now*, Novato, California, New World Library, p. 159.

89. See, www.plato.stanford.edu/entries/emotion/#bib-emotion, last revision January 21, 2013.

90. Mojtabai R., Olfson, M. *Proportion of antidepressants prescribed without a psychiatric diagnosis is growing*, Health Affairs 2011; DOI: 10.1377/hlthaff.2010.1024.

91. Granek, Leeat; O'Rourke, Meghan, *Is Mourning Madness? The wrongheaded movement to classify grief as a mental disorder*; Website: Slate, posted Monday, March 12, 2012 at 6:45 AM ET.

92. Begley, Sharon, *Thomas Reuters 2012*, on-line update 7/13/2012 5:45:52 PM ET.

93. See, *http://www.pewforum.org/2012/12/18/global-religious-landscape-exec/*

94. The Pew Forum on Religion & Public Life, Pew Research Center; *Report 1: Religious Affiliation*, on-line report 10/4/12.

95. Campbell, Joseph, *Thou Art That: Transforming Religious Metaphor*, Novato, CA, New World Library, March 2013, p. 107.

CHAPTER NINE

96. Ecstatic – from a Greek word meaning *to step outside the ordinary*; transcendence from a Latin word meaning *to go beyond*.

97. From Robert Bly's poem *The Horse of Desire*.

98. From Wallace Steven's book *The Poems of Our Climate*.

99. Merriam-Webster at www.merriam-webster.com. Limen, from the Latin word meaning *threshold*. Liminal means (1) of or relating to a sensory threshold, (2) barely perceptible, (3) of, relating to, or being an intermediate state, phase, or condition: in-between, transitional <in the liminal state between life and death . . .>

100. Heller, Nathan; *The New Yorker* magazine, *Little Strangers*. November 19, 2012.

101. *Guidelines for Interreligious Understanding: Points of Agreement or Similarity*, in Joel Verluis, ed., *A Sourcebook for Earth's Community of Religions* (Grand Rapids, MI, CoNexus Press, 1995), 148; and Thomas Keating, *Speaking of Silence*, 126–29, which contains only the guidelines. For simplicity's sake, the later edition found in the *Sourcebook* will be followed. It is a refinement, and in some respects a rewording of the original guidelines.

102. Jean Houston interview with Oprah Winfrey on OWN television program *Soul Sunday*, November 25, 2012.

103. In 2012, the Travis County Dispute Resolution Center hosted a delegation of mediators sponsored by the U.S. Department of State under its International Visitor Leadership Program. The purpose of this gathering was to share information about the practice of mediation in the U.S. and to offer guidance in developing or enhancing mediation practices in their home countries.

104. Civil disputes include non-criminal cases involving contract law, family law (including divorce), employment law, property law, malpractice, etc.

105. Teilhard de Chardin, Pierre, *The Divine Milieu*. Wm. Collins Sons & Co., Ltd., London and Harper & Rowe, New York, 1960.

106. Dobbs, David. *Pacific Standard*, The Social Life of Genes, September/October 2013, Vol. 6/No. 5, pp. 41–49.

107. Ibid.

108. See, www.britannica.com/EBChecked/topic/262934/heredity/50796/DNA-replication-heredity(genetics). See also, on-line videos: www.powershow.com, DNA Replication 1: Basic Mechanism and Enzymology; TEDx Caltech – Drew Berry – Visualization: Biology and Complex Circuits.

109. Mansury, Isabelle M. PhD and Mohanna, Safa.dana.org/Cerebrum/2011/ *Epigenetics and The Human Brain: Where Nurture Meets Nature* @2014 The Dana Foundation.

110. Ibid.

111. Ibid.

112. Bell, Chris, see, http://www.telegraph.co.uk/news/science/10369861/Epigenetics-How-to-alter-your-genes.html

113. Ibid.

114. Mansury, Isabelle M. PhD and Mohanna, Safa.dana.org/Cerebrum/2011/Epigenetics and The Human Brain: Where Nurture Meets Nature @2014 The Dana Foundation.

115. See, www.britannica.com/EBchecked/topic/262934/heredity/50796/DNA-replication-heredity(genetics). See also on-line videos: i.e., www.powershow.com, DNA Replication 1: Basic Mechanism and Enzymology; TEDx Caltech – Drew Berry – visualization: Biology and Complex Circuit.

116. Mansury, Isabelle M. PhD and Mohanna, Safa.dana.org/Cerebrum/2011/ Epigenetics and The Human Brain: Where Nurture Meets Nature @2014 The Dana Foundation.

117. Watters, Ethan. DNA Is Not Destiny: The New Science of Epigenetics, November 22, 2006; found at http://discover magazine.com/2006/Nov.

118. Ibid.

119. Dobbs, David. Pacific Standard: The Social Life of Genes,
September/October 2013, Vol. 6/No. 5, pp. 41–49.

120. See, www.huffingtonpost.com/news/science/dated
10/25/2012.

121. Dobbs, David. Pacific Standard: The Social Life of Genes,
September/October 2013, Vol. 6/No. 5, pp. 41–49.

122. Rohr, Richard. Immortal Diamond, San Francisco, California.
Jossey-Bass, 2013.

ABOUT THE AUTHORS

Attorney, Mediator, Workplace Investigator

With more than thirty years experience in human resource management, law and employee/labor relations, Kathleen claims she had the good fortune of reaching adulthood during the cauldron of the 1960s. Conflict over women's rights, civil rights, race relations and U.S. military interventions in Vietnam and Southeast Asia provoked the development of important diversity initiatives.

A perennial student of behavior and advocate of collaborative systems, Kathleen's work has focused on the power of diversity to build relationships and transform organizations through effective communication and interest-based decision-making, problem solving, training, coaching and dispute resolution. A recognized expert in workplace mediation, Kathleen was invited to speak at the *World Mediation Forum* in Sardinia, Italy.

Mystic, Poet, Writer

When Kathleen's father died three days before her fifth birthday, she began to experience a connection to the mystical nature of the universe that would set the course for her life. Her father's small library included books by Plato, Spinoza, Nietzsche, Shakespeare and Walt Whitman. Reading these great works and a near-death experience at fourteen inspired her to explore the esoteric and begin writing. In her twenties, Kathleen was invited to join a group of mediums as a novitiate where she spent two years studying this psychic phenomenon. Now, in the third trimester of her life, she is committed to making a contribution to understanding the spiritual and co-creative nature of human relationships. An exciting and transformative playground!

Entrepreneur, Executive, Community Leader

For over forty years, Bonner held executive management positions in corporate settings and on community boards. Responsible for the performance and morale of divergent groups, Bonner relied on communication and collaboration to develop emerging organizations and improve understanding. Today, he is working with others to create a dialogue between the dominant and indigenous cultures in Utah, in an effort to preserve core spiritual knowledge, maintain sacred spaces and improve understanding.

Contemplative, Explorer, Shaman

In 2005, upended by divorce and his company's bankruptcy, Bonner experienced a spiritual awakening that altered the course of his life. He returned to an earlier interest in ancient and indigenous people and began a pilgrimage to explore these cultures, with a focus on the concepts of stewardship, order, balance and harmony. Traveling the Nile and the Amazon, through jungles and the high Andes, and in 'walk abouts' in North America's mountains and plains, he gained new perspectives and insights about the history and evolution of humanity. His spiritual development meant setting aside many of the beliefs and patterns of behavior that characterized his *emotional infancy* — a state, he contends, that lasted until he was 57 years old! Bonner's shamanic practices and spiritual anthropology continue to lead him to places of isolation and solitude to read, write and reflect.

www.ingramcontent.com/pod-product-compliance
Lightning Source LLC
Chambersburg PA
CBHW032104280326
41933CB00009B/756

PRAISE FOR *THE OTHERNESS FACTOR*

2015 IPPY AWARD WINNER
Silver Medal | Adult Non-Fiction

Reading *The Otherness Factor* is like having a conversation with the authors. . . . The focus is upon our becoming who we really are, stripping away the *oughts* and *shoulds* that family and society hand to us. . . . for those who are curious, for those who, the authors say, *are always arriving*.
Judith Helburn for Story Circle Book Reviews

. . . a literary effort that transcends the usual pedestrian *pop-psychology* of self-help genre and goes beyond platitudes and clichés. The authors not only invoke the collective wisdom of philosophers, poets, artists and psychologists, but also share their own foibles and vulnerabilities. . . . Authors Hall and Hardegree are the Lewis and Clark of relationships and intentionality. . .
Kenneth Davis, M.D., Author, Speaker

If answered, the writers' call to respect the *otherness* of those with different world views could go far to help resolve the murderous antagonism that seems to be ripping civilizations apart.
Leo McLean, Award-Winning Journalist

. . . through Socratic discussions . . . an approach to life that promotes self-knowledge, liberation from the ego, and an appreciation and acceptance of diversity.
Kirkus Reviews

. . . insightful . . . took me to another level in my understanding of myself and my relationships with other people. . . . For perhaps the first time in my adult life, I was able to put some important relationships into perspective.
Georgia Thomas, M.D., Physician & Professor